AMEN, LIKE THUNDER!!

A Prayer Manual for Extraordinary Breakthroughs

DR. JOHN ANIEMEKE

AMEN LIKE THUNDER!!

Paperback ISBN: 978-1-957809-86-1

Published by Cornerstone Publishing
A Division of Cornerstone Creativity Group LLC
Info@thecornerstonepublishers.com
www.thecornerstonepublishers.com

Author's Contact

To book the author to speak at your next event or to order bulk copies of this book, please, use the information below:

janiemeke@yahoo.com

Printed in the United States of America.

FOREWORD

In a world filled with uncertainties and challenges, prayer remains a powerful, potent, and life-transforming force for seeking divine guidance, solace, divine intervention and solutions. Dr. John Aniemeke's book, "Amen like Thunder," is a comprehensive and revelational guide to prayers loaded with prayer points for various life situations. This book is a valuable resource for anyone seeking to deepen their prayer life and build stronger capacity in the place of prayer.

Dr. John Aniemeke's passion and commitment to the ministry of prayer are evident in this impactful book. Each chapter focuses on a specific topic, providing readers with prayer points to pray. Whether you are facing financial difficulties, health issues, or relationship challenges, "Amen like Thunder" offers prayers that are tailored to your unique situation.

I am confident that "Amen like Thunder" will be a valuable addition to your prayer library. Whether you are a seasoned prayer warrior or someone who is just beginning to explore the world of prayer, this book will inspire and guide you on your spiritual journey. As you delve into its pages, may you find comfort, strength, and hope in the power of prayer, and may your "Amen" resound like thunder, bringing about the manifestation of God's promises in your life.

Benjamin Beckley

Pastor, The Empowerment Center

DEDICATION

To the Almighty God who answer prayer, to You all flesh will come! (Psalm 65:2)

CONTENTS

INTRODUCTION

Welcome to "Amen, Like Thunder: A Prayer Manual for Extraordinary Breakthroughs." This prayer book is designed to be a valuable resource for individuals seeking personal spiritual growth, as well as for church leaders guiding their congregations in prayer.

Whether you are embarking on a personal prayer retreat, engaging in daily devotions, or leading a prayer meeting, this book provides a comprehensive collection of prayers and guidance to support and deepen your prayer life.

Prayer is a divine invitation—an open line of communication with our Creator. It is a privilege and a gift that allows us to express our deepest longings, share our burdens, seek guidance, find comfort, and experience the love and presence of God in our lives. Through prayer, we enter into a sacred space where we can pour out our hearts, listen to God's voice, and align ourselves with His will.

In this prayer book, you will find a collection of heartfelt prayers, carefully crafted to address various aspects of the human experience and the journey of faith. From prayers of thanksgiving and praise to prayers of confession and intercession, each page is an opportunity to encounter God's grace, seek His wisdom, and experience His transforming power.

To guide you in your prayer journey, this book offers prayers for different seasons of life, prayers for specific needs and challenges, prayers for personal growth, and prayers for the community of believers. Additionally, you will find Scripture verses, reflections, and prompts to deepen your understanding of God's Word and inspire your personal reflections.

HOW TO USE THIS PRAYER BOOK:

1. **Set aside dedicated time:** Whether you are using this book individually or leading a group, allocate specific time for prayer and reflection.

2. **Select the appropriate topic:** Choose a topic that aligns with your particular prayer context, whether it's a personal retreat, daily devotion, or church prayer meeting.

3. **Reflect and pray:** Engage with the prayers provided, using them as a starting point for your own conversations with God. Personalize the prayers as you feel led, and allow the Holy Spirit to guide your thoughts and expressions.

4. **Incorporate additional prayers and scriptures:** Feel free to include your personal scriptures, prayer points, intercessions, and specific needs during your prayer

time. This book serves only as a foundation to support and enhance your prayer life. While it contains relevant scriptures needed for prayer, it is not a substitute for the Holy Bible.

5. **Journal and reflect:** Consider keeping a prayer journal to record your thoughts, reflections, and answered prayers. This practice can deepen your spiritual growth and serve as a source of encouragement and gratitude.

1

THANKSGIVING

Psalm 100:4 (NIV)

"Enter his gates with thanksgiving and his courts with praise; give thanks to him and praise his name"

1 Thessalonians 5:18 (NIV)

"Give thanks in all circumstances; for this is God's will for you in Christ Jesus."

Psalm 107:1 (NIV)

"Give thanks to the Lord, for He is good; His love endures forever."

Colossians 3:17 (NIV)

"And whatever you do, whether in word or deed, do it all in the name of the Lord Jesus, giving thanks to God the Father through him."

Ephesians 5:20 (NIV)

"Always giving thanks to God the Father for everything, in the name of our Lord Jesus Christ."

1. Father, I thank You for the precious gift of life. I am grateful for each breath, each day, and the opportunities it brings. Help me to live each day with purpose and gratitude, honoring You in all that I do. May my life be a testimony of Your goodness and love. In Jesus' name, I pray. Amen.
2. Heavenly Father, I am thankful for Your unfailing grace and mercies that are new every morning. I am grateful that Your love and forgiveness are extended to me even when I fall short. I thank You for the gift of salvation and the opportunity to experience Your grace in my life.
3. Heavenly Father, I thank You for the gift of family. I am grateful for the love, support, and unity that we share. I pray for Your continued blessings upon my family, that You would strengthen our bonds and guide us in walking in Your ways.
4. Lord, I am thankful for the opportunities and successes in my career. I acknowledge that every good thing comes from You, and I give thanks for the skills, talents, and opportunities You have provided. Help me to use my career to glorify You and make a positive impact in the lives of others.
5. Father, I thank You for Your constant protection over my life. I am grateful for Your watchful eye and Your

deliverance from danger and harm. I pray for Your continued protection over me, my loved ones, and all that concerns me.

6. Lord, I give thanks for the strength You provide in times of weakness and the provision You supply in times of need. I am grateful for Your faithfulness and provision in all areas of my life. I trust in Your continued provision and ask for Your wisdom in managing all that You have entrusted to me.

7. Lord, I lift up the church and its leadership before You in gratitude. Thank You for the spiritual guidance, teaching, and support they provide. I pray for Your wisdom and anointing to rest upon the leaders, that they may lead with integrity, humility, and the power of Your Spirit. In Jesus' name, I pray. Amen.

2
REPENTANCE

1 John 1:9 (NIV)

"If we confess our sins, He is faithful and just to forgive us our sins and cleanse us from all unrighteousness."

Psalm 51:10 (NIV)

"Create in me a pure heart, O God, and renew a steadfast spirit within me."

Psalm 51:7 (NIV)

"Cleanse me with hyssop, and I will be clean; wash me, and Iwill be whiter than snow."

Acts 3:19 (NIV)

"Repent, then, and turn to God, so that your sins may be wiped out, that times of refreshing may come from the Lord."

2 Chronicles 7:14 (NIV)

"If my people, who are called by my name, will humble themselves and pray and seek my face and turn from their wicked ways, then I will hear from heaven, and I will forgive their sin and will heal their land."

1. Heavenly Father, please forgive me for the times when I have sinned against You knowingly or unknowingly. Help me to recognize my faults and shortcomings and turn away from them.

2. Lord, I confess that I have sinned against You and against others. Help me to seek forgiveness from those whom I have wronged and to make things right with them.

3. God, Lord, cleanse me with hyssop and wash me thoroughly from my iniquity. I pray that You would make me whiter than snow and remove any stains of sin that cling to me.

4. Lord, create in me a clean heart and renew a right spirit within me. Remove any pride, selfishness, or unforgiveness that may be hindering my relationship with You.

5. Father, I acknowledge that my sins have separated me from You, and I repent of my wrongdoing. Please restore to me the joy of Your salvation and grant me a willing spirit to follow You.

6. Father, I ask for Your grace and mercy to cover me as I repent of my sins. I trust in Your unfailing love and ask that You would blot out my transgressions and remember my sins no more.

7. Holy Spirit, help me to walk in the path of righteousness and to avoid the temptations of the evil one. Strengthen me in my resolve to turn away from sin and to pursue a life of holiness and obedience to Your will. In Jesus' name, I pray. Amen.

3

HINDRANCES TO PRAYER

Psalm 66:18 (NIV)

"If I had cherished sin in my heart, the Lord would not have listened."

James 4:3 (NIV)

"When you ask, you do not receive, because you ask with wrong motives, that you may spend what you get on your pleasures."

James 1:6-7 (NIV)

"But when you ask, you must believe and not doubt, because the one who doubts is like a wave of the sea, blown and tossed by the wind. That person should not expect to receive anything from the Lord."

Proverbs 28:9 (NIV)

"If anyone turns a deaf ear to my instructions, even their prayers are detestable."

Matthew 6:6 (NIV)

"But when you pray, go into your room, close the door and pray to your Father, who is unseen. Then your Father, who sees what is done in secret, will reward you."

1. Father, in the name of Jesus, I come before Your throne of grace, and I bind every hindrance that seeks to block my prayers from reaching You.
2. Lord, I confess any sins that may be hindering my prayers and ask for Your forgiveness. I plead the blood of Jesus over my life and my prayers, and I rebuke every demonic force that would try to thwart my prayers.
3. Heavenly Father, I pray that You would remove any doubt, unbelief, or lack of faith that may be hindering my prayers. Help me to trust in Your promises and to pray with boldness and confidence.
4. Lord, break every stronghold that is hindering my prayers. I renounce every negative word spoken over my life, and I declare that I am an overcomer in Christ Jesus.
5. Father, I pray that You would give me a spirit of humility and a contrite heart. Help me to seek Your will and not my own desires, so that my prayers may be aligned with Your purpose.

6. Lord, please remove any distractions or busyness that may be hindering me from spending time in prayer. Help me to prioritize my relationship with You above all else.
7. Holy Spirit, I pray that You would intercede for me according to Your will and help me to pray in accordance with Your promptings. I trust in Your guidance and seek to pray in alignment with Your purposes for my life. Amen.

4
DELIVERANCE

Psalm 34:17 (NIV)
"The righteous cry out, and the Lord hears them; He delivers them from all their troubles."

Nahum 1:7 (NIV)
"The Lord is good, a refuge in times of trouble. He cares for those who trust in Him."

Psalm 50:15 (NIV)
"Call on me in the day of trouble; I will deliver you, and you will honor me."

Psalm 105:37 (NIV)
"He brought them forth also with silver and gold: and there was not one feeble person among their tribes."

Exodus 14:13-14 (NIV)
"Do not be afraid. Stand still, and see the salvation of the Lord, which He will accomplish for you today. For the Egyptians whom you see today, you shall see again no more forever. The Lord will fight for you, and you shall hold your peace"

1. Heavenly Father, I thank You for the ways in which You have already delivered me and provided for me in the past, and for the promise of overflowing blessings that You have for me in the future.
2. Lord, please give me the grace to trust in Your faithfulness and provision in every area of my life, even when circumstances seem uncertain or difficult.
3. Father, please show me any areas of my life where I may be in need of deliverance, whether it be physical, emotional, or spiritual, and help me to surrender those areas to You.
4. Lord, give me the courage and strength to take any necessary steps to receive the deliverance that You have for me, whether it involves seeking help from others, confessing sin, or letting go of unhealthy patterns or relationships.
5. Father, I declare Your promises of deliverance and abundance over my life, believing that You are able to do immeasurably more than I can ask or imagine.
6. Lord, please fill my heart with a spirit of generosity and gratitude, so that I may overflow with Your love and blessings to those around me.

7.

8. Father, Lord, use my life and testimony of deliverance to bring glory to Your name and to be a blessing to others who are in need of Your saving grace. May Your goodness and mercy follow me all the days of my life, and may I dwell in Your house forever. In Jesus' name, I pray. Amen.

5

SIGNS AND WONDERS BY THE HOLY SPIRIT

Acts 1:8 (NIV)

"But you will receive power when the Holy Spirit comes on you; and you will be my witnesses in Jerusalem, and in all Judea and Samaria, and to the ends of the earth."

Mark 16:17-18 (NIV)

"And these signs will accompany those who believe: In my name they will drive out demons; they will speak in new tongues; they will pick up snakes with their hands; and when they drink deadly poison, it will not hurt them at all; they will place their hands on sick people, and they will get well."

Hebrews 2:4 (NIV)

"God also testified to it by signs, wonders and various miracles, and by gifts of the Holy Spirit distributed according to his will."

John 14:12 (NIV)

"Very truly I tell you, whoever believes in me will do the works I have been doing, and they will do even greater things than these, because I am going to the Father."

Acts 2:43 (NIV)

"Everyone was filled with awe at the many wonders and sings performed by the apostles."

1. Heavenly Father, I thank You for the power of Your Holy Spirit, and for the ways in which You have already worked signs and wonders in my life.
2. Lord, I pray that You would fill me afresh with Your Holy Spirit, and empower me to be a vessel for Your signs and wonders in the world around me.
3. Father, I pray that You would increase my faith and trust in Your power, and that I would not limit what You are able to do through me.
4. Lord, I ask for a deeper understanding of Your plans and purposes, so that I may be able to discern the signs and wonders that You are working in my life and the lives of those around me.
5. Father, I declare that no weapon formed against me shall prosper, and that the signs and wonders of Your Holy Spirit will be evident in every area of my life.

6. Lord, I pray that You would use me to bring hope and healing to those who are hurting and in need of a touch from You, and that Your signs and wonders would be a testimony to Your love and faithfulness.
7. Father, I thank You for the privilege of being called Your child, and I pray that I would live my life in such a way that others would see the signs and wonders of Your Holy Spirit in me, and be drawn closer to You as a result. In Jesus' name, Amen.

6

WONDER TO MANY

Psalm 139:14 (NIV)

"I praise You because I am fearfully and wonderfully made; Your works are wonderful, I know that full well."

Psalm 71:7-8 (NIV)

"I have become a wonder to many, For You are my strong refuge. My mouth is filled with Your praise and with Your glory all day long."

Isaiah 8:18 (NIV)

"Behold, I and the children whom the LORD hath given me are for signs and for wonders in Israel from the LORD of hosts, which dwelleth in mount Zion."

1 Corinthians 4:9 (NIV)

"For I think that God hath set forth us the apostles last, as it were appointed to death: for we are made a spectacle unto the world, and to angels, and to men."

Matthew 5:16 (NIV)

"in the same way, let your light shine before others, that they may see your good deeds and glorify your Father in heaven."

1. Heavenly Father, I thank You for creating me fearfully and wonderfully, and for the unique gifts and talents that You have given me.
2. Lord, I pray that You would help me to see myself the way that You see me, and to embrace the wonder and beauty of who I am in You.
3. Father, I pray that You would use my life as a testimony to Your goodness and faithfulness, and that I would be a wonder to many as they see Your hand at work in me.
4. Lord, I pray for the courage to step out in faith and use the gifts that You have given me to make a difference in the world around me.
5. Father, I ask for the humility to recognize that any wonder or greatness in me comes from You alone, and to give You all the glory and honor for what You are able to do through me.
6. Lord, I pray for the discernment to recognize opportunities to be a wonder to others, and for the willingness to step out of my comfort zone and take risks for Your sake.
7. Father, Lord, continue to shape and mold me into the person that You have created me to be, so that I may be a wonder to many and bring glory to Your name. In Jesus' name, Amen.

7

MIRACLES

Matthew 19:26 (NIV)

"Jesus looked at them and said, "With man this is impossible, but with God all things are possible."

Mark 9:23-24 (NIV)

"And Jesus said to him, 'If you can! All things are possible for one who believes.' Immediately the father of the child cried out and said, 'I believe; help my unbelief!"

Psalm 77:14 (NIV)

"You are the God who performs miracles; You display Your power among the peoples."

1 John 5:14-15 (NIV)

"And this is the confidence that we have toward him, that if we ask anything according to his will he hears us. And if we know that he hears us in whatever we ask, we know that we have the requests that we have asked of him."

Jeremiah 32:27 (NIV)

"I am the Lord, the God of all mankind. Is anything too hard for me?"

1. Heavenly Father, I thank You for the opportunity to experience a raw miracle, and for the ways in which You have already worked miracles in my life.
2. Father, I declare that no situation is too difficult for You to handle, and that all things are possible through You. I ask for the faith to believe in Your power to work miracles in my life and the lives of those around me.
3. Lord, I pray that You would open my heart and mind to receive all that You have for me, and that I would be fully surrendered to Your will and purposes.
4. Lord, I pray for a fresh outpouring of Your Holy Spirit and a deeper intimacy with You as I seek after You with all my heart.
5. Lord, I pray for healing in every area of my life - physical, emotional, and spiritual - and for the courage to step out in faith and receive all You have for me.
6. Father, Lord, work in me and through me to bring glory to Your name, and may the miracles that take place be a testimony to Your power and love.
7. Father, I thank You in advance for the miracles that will take place in my life, and for the ways in which You will use them to bring about transformation in my life and in the lives of those around me. In Jesus' name, Amen.

8

DIVINE HEALING

Psalm 103:2-3 (NIV)

"Bless the Lord, O my soul, and forget not all his benefits, who forgives all your iniquity, who heals all your diseases."

Psalm 147:3 (NIV)

"He heals the brokenhearted and binds up their wounds."

Jeremiah 17:14 (NIV)

"Heal me, Lord, and I will be healed; save me and I will be saved, for you are the one I praise."

James 5:15 (NIV)

"And the prayer offered in faith will make the sick person well; the Lord will raise them up. If they have sinned, they will be forgiven."

Jeremiah 30:17 (NIV)

"But I will restore you to health and heal your wounds,' declares the Lord, 'because you are called an outcast, Zion for whom no one cares."

1. Heavenly Father, I come to You in faith, believing that You are a God who heals. Please heal me of every sickness, disease, and affliction that I am facing.
2. Lord, I pray that You would heal me not just physically, but also emotionally and spiritually. Lord, bring healing to every area of my life that needs it.
3. Father, I declare that I am not too broken or too far gone for Your healing touch. Please meet me right where I am and bring complete restoration to my body, mind, and spirit.
4. Lord, I pray for the faith to trust in Your healing power, even when my circumstances seem overwhelming. Help me to fix my eyes on You and not on my problems.
5. Father, I ask for the wisdom to take care of my body and to make healthy choices that will promote healing. Help me to partner with You in my own healing process.
6. Lord, I pray for those who are also in need of healing. Lord, touch them with Your healing power and bring them the same restoration that You are bringing to me.
7. Father, I thank You for the promise of healing in Psalm 147:3. I trust in Your goodness and love, and I believe that You are able to do far more than I could ask or imagine. In Jesus' name, Amen.

9

SPEEDY RECOVERY

Jeremiah 30:17 (NIV)

"But I will restore you to health and heal your wounds,' declares the Lord.."

Isaiah 40:31 (NIV)

"But those who hope in the Lord will renew their strength. They will soar on wings like eagles; they will run and not grow weary, they will walk and not be faint.."

2 Corinthians 12:9 (NIV)

"But he said to me, 'My grace is sufficient for you, for my power is made perfect in weakness.' Therefore I will boast all the more gladly of my weaknesses, so that the power of Christ may rest upon me."

Ephesians 3:16 (NIV)

"I pray that out of his glorious riches he may strengthen you with power through his Spirit in your inner being."

Philippians 4:13 (NIV)

"I can do all things through him who gives me strength."

1. Gracious God, I come before You today with a humble and contrite heart, asking for Your help in recovering from any ailment or setback that may be hindering me. Give me the strength to overcome and achieve great things through Your power.

2. Father, I declare that no challenge or obstacle will stand in the way of my recovery or success. With Your help, I know that I can overcome any difficulty and achieve great things.

3. Father, I ask for Your wisdom and discernment as I make decisions about my recovery and goals. Guide me in the right direction and help me to make choices that honor You and bring me success.

4. Heavenly Father, Lord, provide me with the resources and opportunities I need to accomplish my goals. I trust that Your plans for me are good and that You will lead me to success.

5. Lord, I know that I am not strong enough on my own to accomplish all that I desire, but I trust that You will give me the strength to persevere and succeed. Help me to lean on You and rely on Your guidance in all that I do.

6. Lord, I pray for patience and endurance as I work towards my recovery and goals. Help me to stay focused and committed to my goals, even when the journey seems long and difficult.

7. Lord, I thank You for the promise of Philippians 4:13, which assures me that I can do all things through You who strengthens me. I trust in Your power and provision for my life, and I believe that with Your help, I can accomplish great things. In Jesus' name, Amen.

10

MIGHTY DELIVERANCE

Psalm 18:2 (NIV)

"The Lord is my rock, my fortress and my deliverer; my God is my rock, in whom I take refuge, my shield and the horn of my salvation, my stronghold."

Psalm 18:19 (NIV)

"He brought me out into a broad place; he rescued me, because he delighted in me."

Isaiah 54:17 (NIV)

" No weapon forged against you will prevail, and you will refute every tongue that accuses you. This is the heritage of the servants of the Lord, and this is their vindication from me," declares the Lord.."

2 Timothy 4:18 (NIV)

"The Lord will rescue me from every evil deed and bring me safely into his heavenly kingdom. To him be the glory forever and ever. Amen."

Psalm 34:17 (NIV)

"The righteous cry out, and the Lord hears them; He delivers them from all their troubles."

1. Heavenly Father, I come to You today with a grateful heart, thanking You for Your mighty deliverance in my life. You are my rock, my fortress, and my deliverer, and I trust in Your power to protect and rescue me from every danger and trouble.
2. Lord, I confess that there are times when I feel weak and helpless, but I know that You are my source of strength and courage. Help me to lean on You and take refuge in Your presence, knowing that You are my shield and the horn of my salvation.
3. Father, I declare that no weapon formed against me shall prosper, and every tongue that rises against me in judgment will be condemned. I am confident in Your power to deliver me from every attack of the enemy.
4. Lord, I pray for Your mighty deliverance in every area of my life. Help me to overcome every obstacle and challenge that comes my way, and guide me on the path of righteousness and truth.
5. Lord, I pray for Your protection and provision over my family, friends, and loved ones. Surround them with Your love and grace, and shield them from every danger and harm.
6. Father, Lord, make me sensitive to Your voice and promptings, so that I may follow Your lead and walk in Your ways. Grant me the wisdom to discern Your will and the courage to obey.

7. Father, I thank You for your promise of mighty deliverance in Psalm 18:2. I trust in Your power and provision for my life, and I believe that with Your help, I can overcome every obstacle and achieve great things. In Jesus' name, Amen.

11

BREAKTHROUGHS

Isaiah 58:8 (NIV)

"Then your light will break forth like the dawn, and your healing will quickly appear; then your righteousness will go before you, and the glory of the Lord will be your rear guard."

Micah 2:13 (NIV)

" The One who breaks open the way will go up before them; they will break through the gate and go out. Their King will pass through before them, the Lord at their head.."

2 Samuel 5:20 (NIV)

" So David went to Baal Perazim, and there he defeated them. He said, 'As waters break out, the Lord has broken out against my enemies before me.' So that place was called Baal Perazim."

Isaiah 43:19 (NIV)

"For I am about to do something new. See, I have already begun! Do you not see it? I will make a pathway through the wilderness. I will create rivers in the dry wasteland."

Psalm 37:4 (NIV)

"Delight yourself in the Lord, and he will give you the desires of your heart."

1. Lord, I thank You for the promise of breakthroughs in Isaiah 58:8. I know that with You, all things are possible, and I trust in Your power and provision for my life.
2. Father, Lord, help me to turn away from sin and seek You with all my heart. I know that breakthroughs come when I walk in obedience and faith, and I pray that You would help me to do just that.
3. Lord, I pray for breakthroughs in my relationships, my finances, my health, and every other area of my life. I know that You are a God of abundance and that You have good things in store for me.
4. Lord, I pray that Your righteousness would go before me and prepare the way for breakthroughs in every area of my life. Help me to trust in Your goodness and provision, and to follow Your lead on the path of righteousness.
5. Father, Lord, pour out Your glory upon me and be my rear guard, protecting me from every attack of the enemy. I believe that with You by my side, I can overcome any obstacle and achieve great things

6. Father, Lord, give me the strength and courage to persevere in the face of adversity, knowing that breakthroughs are possible through You. Help me to keep my eyes fixed on You and to trust in Your promises.
7. Lord, I come before You today with a heart that is hungry for breakthroughs in my life. I pray that Your light would break forth like the dawn in my life, bringing healing, transformation, and hope. In Jesus' name, I pray. Amen.

12

OPEN DOORS

Revelation 3:8 (NIV)

"I know your deeds. See, I have placed before you an open door that no one can shut. I know that you have little strength, yet you have kept my word and have not denied my name."

Isaiah 22:22 (NIV)

"I will place on his shoulder the key to the house of David; what he opens no one can shut, and what he shuts no one can open."

Matthew 7:7-8 (NIV)

"Ask, and it will be given to you; seek, and you will find; knock, and it will be opened to you. For everyone who asks receives, and the one who seeks finds, and to the one who knocks it will be opened."

Colossians 4:3 (NIV)

"And pray for us, too, that God may open a door for our message, so that we may proclaim the mystery of Christ, for which I am in chains."

1 Corinthians 16:9 (NIV)

"For a great door and effectual is opened unto me, and there are many adversaries."

1. Father, I thank You for the promise of open doors in Your Word. I know that You are faithful to fulfill Your promises, and I trust that the doors You have opened for me will lead to blessings beyond my wildest dreams.
2. Lord, I know that You are the God of open doors, and that no one can shut the doors that You have opened for me. I pray that You would help me to recognize these doors when they appear, and that I would walk through them with confidence and boldness.
3. Father, I come before You today with a heart that is open to the opportunities You have in store for me. I pray that You would guide me to the doors that You have opened for me, and that I would have the courage to step through them in faith.
4. Lord, I pray that You would give me the wisdom and discernment to recognize the difference between doors that You have opened and doors that lead to destruction. Help me to seek Your guidance in every decision I make, and to choose the path that leads to life.
5. Father, Lord, prepare me for the opportunities that You have in store for me. Help me to develop the skills and character that I need to succeed in the doors that You have opened.
6. Lord, I pray that You would use the open doors in my life to bring glory to Your name. May I be a witness to

Your grace and goodness, and may others be drawn to You through the opportunities You have given me.

7. Father, Lord, remove any fear or doubt that may be holding me back from walking through the open doors that You have placed before me. Help me to trust in Your provision and to believe that You have good things in store for me. In Jesus' name, I pray. Amen.

13

REVIVAL OF THE SPIRIT MAN

Psalm 85:6 (NIV)

"Will you not revive us again, that your people may rejoice in you?"

Ezekiel 36:26-27 (NIV)

"I will give you a new heart and put a new spirit in you; I will remove from you your heart of stone and give you a heart of flesh. And I will put my Spirit in you and move you to follow my decrees and be careful to keep my laws."

Isaiah 57:15 (NIV)

"For thus says the high and exalted One who lives forever, whose name is Holy, "I dwell on a high and holy place, and also with the contrite and lowly of spirit in order to revive the spirit of the lowly and to revive the heart of the contrite."

Romans 8:11 (NIV)

"And if the Spirit of him who raised Jesus from the dead is living in you, he who raised Christ from the dead will also give life to your mortal bodies because of his Spirit who lives in you."

Psalm 51:10 (NIV)

"Create in me a pure heart, O God, and renew a steadfast spirit within me."

1. Heavenly Father, I come to You with a heart that longs for revival. Lord revive my spirit and draw me closer to You.
2. Lord, I acknowledge that I am weak and in need of Your strength. I pray that You would pour out Your Holy Spirit upon me and empower me to live a life that is pleasing to You.
3. Father, Lord, search my heart and reveal to me any areas of sin or disobedience. I pray that You would forgive me and cleanse me from all unrighteousness.
4. Lord, I surrender my will to Yours and ask that You would lead me in the paths of righteousness. I pray that You would help me to obey Your commands and to follow Your ways.
5. Father, I pray that You would renew my passion for You and give me a hunger for Your Word. Help me to delight in Your presence and to seek You with all my heart.
6. Lord, I pray for a fresh anointing of Your Spirit in my life. Lord fill me with Your love, joy, peace, patience, kindness, goodness, faithfulness, gentleness, and self-control.

7. Father, I thank You for the promise of revival in Your Word. I trust that You will revive my spirit and restore me to a right relationship with You. May my life be a living testimony of Your grace and love. In Jesus' name, Amen.

14

SUPERNATURAL STRENGTH

Isaiah 40:29-31 (NIV)

"He giveth power to the faint; and to them that have no might he increaseth strength. Even the youths shall faint and be weary, and the young men shall utterly fall. But they that wait upon the Lord shall renew their strength; they shall mount up with wings as eagles; they shall run, and not be weary; and they shall walk, and not faint."

Isaiah 41:10 (NIV)

"So do not fear, for I am with you; do not be dismayed, for I am your God. I will strengthen you and help you; I will uphold you with my righteous right hand."

Psalms 18:28-29 (NIV)

"You, Lord, keep my lamp burning; my God turns my darkness into light. With your help I can advance against a troop; with my God I can scale a wall."

Philippians 4:13 (NIV)

"I can do all things through Christ which strengtheneth me."

2 Corinthians 12:9 (NIV)

" But he said to me, 'My grace is sufficient for you, for my power is made perfect in weakness.' Therefore I will boast all the more gladly about my weaknesses, so that Christ's power may rest on me."

1. Heavenly Father, I come before You today asking for supernatural strength. I pray that You will give me the strength I need to face the challenges that lie ahead.
2. Lord, I acknowledge that I am weak and in need of Your help. I pray that You would renew my strength and give me the energy I need to accomplish all that You have called me to do.
3. Father, please help me wait upon You and trust in Your timing. I pray that You would renew my hope and give me the courage to press on in faith.
4. Lord, I pray that You would help me to soar on wings like eagles, to run and not grow weary, to walk and not faint. Lord enable me to rise above the challenges of life and to be a witness of Your power and strength.
5. Father, I pray that You would give me a hunger for Your Word and a thirst for Your presence. Lord, fill me with Your Spirit and enable me to live a life that brings glory to Your name.
6. Lord, I pray that You would help me to focus on You and not on my circumstances. Lord, give me a supernatural peace that surpasses all understanding and guards my heart and mind in Christ Jesus.

7. Father, I thank You for the promise of supernatural strength in Your Word. I trust that You will uphold me with Your righteous right hand and that nothing can separate me from Your love. In Jesus' name, Amen.

15

MANIFESTATION OF GLORY

Isaiah 60:1-2 (NIV)

"Arise, shine; for your light has come, And the glory of the LORD has risen upon you. For behold, darkness will cover the earth and deep darkness the peoples; but the Lord will rise upon you and His glory will appear upon you."

Isaiah 40: 4-5 (NIV)

"Every valley shall be exalted, and every mountain and hill shall be made low: and the crooked shall be made straight, and the rough places plain: And the glory of the Lord shall be revealed, and all flesh shall see it together: for the mouth of the Lord hath spoken it."

2 Cointhians 3:18 (NIV)

"And we all, who with unveiled faces contemplate the Lord's glory, are being transformed into his image with ever-increasing glory, which comes from the Lord, who is the Spirit."

John 17:22 (NIV)

"I have given them the glory that you gave me, that they may be one as we are one."

Romans 3:23 (NIV)

"For all have sinned and fall short of the glory of God."

1. Heavenly Father, I come before You today asking for Your glory to manifest in my life. I pray that Your light will shine upon me and that Your glory would be seen in everything that I do.
2. Lord, I thank You for the promise of Isaiah 60:1-2, that Your glory will arise upon me and that the nations will be drawn to Your light. I pray that I would be a beacon of Your love and grace, shining brightly for all to see.
3. Father, please remove any obstacles or barriers that are hindering thc manifestation of Your glory in my life. I pray that I would be fully surrendered to You and that You would have complete control over every area of my life.
4. Lord, I pray that You would help me to live a life that is pleasing to You. Give me the wisdom and discernment I need to make decisions that honor You and bring glory to Your name.
5. Father, I pray that You would fill me with Your Holy Spirit and empower me to do Your will. I ask that You use me to bring hope and healing to those around me and that Your glory is revealed through me.
6. Lord, I pray that You would help me to keep my eyes fixed on You and not on the things of this world. Lord,

give me a heart that is fully devoted to You and that Your glory would be the driving force behind everything that I do.

7. Father, I thank you for the promise of Isaiah 40:4-5, that every valley shall be lifted up and every mountain and hill made low, and the glory of the Lord shall be revealed. I pray that Your glory will be revealed in my life in a powerful way, and that many would come to know You as a result. In Jesus' name, Amen.

16

DIVINE FAVOR

Psalm 102:13 (NIV)

"You will arise and have compassion on Zion, for it is time to show favor to her; the appointed time has come."

Psalm 106:4 (NIV)

"Remember me, O LORD, in Your favor toward Your people; visit me with Your salvation."

Psalms 90:17 (NIV)

"May the favor of the Lord our God rest upon us; establish the work of our hands for us— yes, establish the work of our hands."

Psalm 5:12 (NIV)

"Surely, Lord you bless the righteous; you surround them with your favor as with a shield."

Psalms 90:17 (NIV)

" And Jesus grew in wisdom and stature, and in favor with God and man."

1. Heavenly Father, I come before You today and ask for Your divine favor to be upon my life. I pray that Your grace and mercy would surround me, and that Your favor would open doors that no man can shut.
2. Lord, I thank You for the promise of Psalm 106:4, that You will show favor to those who love You and keep Your commandments. I pray that I would love You with all my heart, soul, mind, and strength, and that I would keep Your commandments always.
3. Father, Lord, bless the work of my hands and grant me success in all that I do. I pray that Your favor would be upon me in my career, my relationships, and every area of my life.
4. Lord, I pray that You would give me a heart of wisdom and understanding and that You would guide me in the path that You have for me. Let Your favor lead me to the places where You want me to be, and open doors for me that no one can shut.
5. Father, I pray that You would make me a vessel of Your grace and mercy, and that Your favor would flow through me to others. Lord, use me to bless those around me, and let Your love be evident in all that I say and do.
6. Lord, I thank You for the promise of Psalm 90:17, that Your favor would rest upon us and establish the work

of our hands. I pray that Your favor would be upon me and that You would establish the work of my hands for Your glory.

7. Father, Lord, give me a heart that is fully surrendered to You, and help me to seek first Your kingdom and Your righteousness. I pray that Your favor would be upon me as I seek to do Your will, and that You would use me to bring glory to Your name. In Jesus' name, Amen.

17

DIVINE CONSOLIDATION

Zechariah 8:12 (NIV)

"The seed will grow well, the vine will yield its fruit, the ground will produce its crops, and the heavens will drop their dew. I will give all these things as an inheritance to the remnant of this people."

Philippians 1:6 (NIV)

"Being confident of this, that he who began a good work in you will carry it on to completion until the day of Christ Jesus."

Psalm 37:23-24 (NIV)

"The Lord makes firm the steps of the one who delights in him; though he may stumble, he will not fall, for the Lord upholds him with his hand."

2 Corinthians 9:8 (NIV)

"And God is able to bless you abundantly, so that in all things at all times, having all that you need, you will abound in every good work."

Psalm 138:8 (NIV)

"The Lord will fulfill his purpose for me; your love, O Lord, endures forever—do not abandon the works of your hands."

1. Heavenly Father, I thank You for the promise of divine consolidation over my life according to Your Word in Zechariah 8:12. I declare that I am rooted and established in You, and I will not be moved by the storms of life.
2. Lord, I pray for divine consolidation in every area of my life - my career, my relationships, my health, and my spiritual life. May You strengthen me and give me the grace to endure any trial or challenge that comes my way.
3. I declare that the work that You have begun in me, Lord, You will complete it until the day of Jesus Christ, according to Philippians 1:6. I trust in Your unfailing love and the power of Your Holy Spirit to guide me towards completion.
4. Father, Lord, establish me in righteousness and grant me the wisdom and discernment to make the right decisions. May Your hand be upon my life, leading me in the paths of righteousness and divine destiny.
5. I pray for divine connections and opportunities that would lead to my consolidation and advancement in life. May I be at the right place at the right time and connect with the right people who will help me fulfill my purpose and destiny.

6. I reject any form of setback or stagnation in my life, and I receive divine acceleration and consolidation. I declare that I am moving forward, and nothing can hinder or delay my progress.
7. Lord, I thank You for Your faithfulness and for keeping me in the center of Your will. I pray for divine consolidation in my life, family, and every area of my existence, in Jesus' name. Amen.

18

GREATNESS

Jeremiah 29:11 (NIV)

For I know the plans I have for you," declares the Lord, "plans to prosper you and not to harm you, plans to give you hope and a future.

Psalm 71:21 (NIV)

"Thou shalt increase my greatness, And comfort me on every side."

Psalm 18:35 (NIV)

"You make your saving help my shield, and your right hand sustains me; your help has made me great."

Isaiah 60:22 (NIV)

"The least of you will become a thousand, the smallest a mighty nation. I am the Lord; in its time I will do this swiftly."

Genesis 26:12-14 (NIV)

"Then Isaac sowed in that land, and received in the same year an hundredfold: and the LORD blessed him. And the man waxed great, and went forward, and grew until he became very great: for he had possession of flocks, and possession of herds, and great store of servants: and the Philistines envied him."

1. Heavenly Father, I thank You for Your promise of divine greatness over my life, according to Your Word in Jeremiah 29:11. I declare that You have great plans for my life, plans to prosper me and not to harm me, plans to give me hope and a future.
2. Lord, I pray for a greater revelation of Your love and grace in my life. May I understand the depth and height of Your love and live my life in accordance with Your will.
3. I pray for divine wisdom and knowledge, that I may be able to discern Your voice and follow Your guidance. May I have a heart that seeks after You, and a mind that is set on the things of the Spirit.
4. I ask that You help me to live a life of humility, putting others before myself and always seeking to serve and bless others. May Your character of love and kindness be reflected in my life, so that others may see and glorify You.
5. Lord, I pray for divine favor and blessings in every area of my life. May Your hand be upon me, leading me towards success and prosperity, according to Your will.
6. I declare that I am an overcomer through Christ who strengthens me, and I will not be overcome by any challenge or obstacle that comes my way. May Your Spirit empower me to walk in divine greatness and victory in every season of my life.

7. Finally, I pray for a deeper intimacy with You, Lord, that I may know You more and experience Your presence and power in my life. May Your glory be made manifest in and through me, that others may be drawn to You and come to experience the greatness of Your love. In Jesus' name, Amen.

19

DIVINE ESTABLISHMENT

Psalm 90:17 (NIV)

"May the favor of the Lord our God rest on us; establish the work of our hands for us—yes, establish the work of our hands."

Isaiah 54:13-14 (NIV)

"All your sons will be taught of the LORD; And the well-being of your sons will be great. In righteousness you will be established."

1 Peter 5:10 (NIV)

But may the God of all grace, who called us to His eternal glory by Christ Jesus, after you have suffered a while, perfect, establish, strengthen, and settle you.

Psalm 37:23-24 (NIV)

"The Lord makes firm the steps of the one who delights in him; though he may stumble, he will not fall, for the Lord upholds him with his hand."

Isaiah 33:6 (NIV)

"He will be the sure foundation for your times, a rich store of salvation and wisdom and knowledge; the fear of the Lord is the key to this treasure."

1. Lord, I declare that I am rooted and grounded in You. Let my faith in You be unshakable and unwavering, even in the midst of trials and challenges.
2. Holy Spirit, help me to walk in obedience to Your voice and guidance. May I never be swayed by the opinions of others or the distractions of this world.
3. Father, I pray for supernatural wisdom and understanding to navigate through life's complexities and make wise decisions that align with Your plan for my life.
4. Dear God, I thank You for Your unwavering faithfulness and love towards me. Please establish me in my career, business, relationships, and every area of my life according to Your perfect will.
5. Lord, I pray for divine connections that will propel me towards my destiny. May I encounter individuals who will help me to achieve my goals and fulfill my purpose.
6. Heavenly Father, I ask that You establish me in good health and sound mind. May my body, soul, and spirit be strengthened to fulfill all that You have called me to do.
7. Gracious God, I pray for divine provision in all areas of my life. May Your abundance flow into my finances, resources, and every need that I have. May I always be a channel of blessing to others as You establish me for Your glory. In Jesus' name, Amen.

20

DIVINE FIRE & POWER

2 Peter 1:3 (NIV)

"Seeing that His divine power has granted to us everything pertaining to life and godliness, through the true knowledge of Him who called us by His own glory and excellence."

Acts 1:8 (NIV)

"But you will receive power when the Holy Spirit comes on you; and you will be my witnesses in Jerusalem, and in all Judea and Samaria, and to the ends of the earth."

Ephesians 3:16 (NIV)

" I pray that out of his glorious riches he may strengthen you with power through his Spirit in your inner being."

2 Timothy 1:7 (NIV)

" For the Spirit God gave us does not make us timid, but gives us power, love, and self-discipline."

Hebrews 12:29 (NIV)

"For our God is a consuming fire."

1. Heavenly Father, I thank You for Your promise of divine power through the Holy Spirit. I pray that Your power would be made manifest in my life in ways that bring You glory.
2. Lord, I ask for an increase in Your power to evangelize and share the gospel boldly and effectively. May Your Spirit empower me to be a witness for You in all areas of my life.
3. Father, I pray for supernatural power to overcome every obstacle and challenge that I may face. May Your power be made perfect in my weakness, and may I trust in Your strength and not my own.
4. Gracious God, I pray for Your power to be at work in my ministry and service to others. May I be a vessel for Your power and love to flow through, bringing healing, deliverance, and salvation to those in need. In Jesus' name, I pray. Amen.
5. Heavenly Father, I ask for Your power to be evident in my personal growth and spiritual development. May I continually be transformed by Your Spirit and become more like Jesus.
6. Holy Spirit, I ask for Your power to be at work in my prayer life. May I be led by Your Spirit to pray according to Your will and see miraculous answers to my prayers.

7. Lord, I pray for Your power to be at work in my relationships, both with believers and non-believers. May Your love and power be evident in the way that I interact with others. In Jesus' name, I pray. Amen.

21

VICTORY OVER SICKNESS AND DEATH

Isaiah 53:5 (NIV)

"But he was pierced for our transgressions, he was crushed for our iniquities; the punishment that brought us peace was on him, and by his wounds we are healed."

Psalm 118:17 (NIV)

" I will not die but live, and will proclaim what the Lord has done."

John 11:4 (NIV)

"But when Jesus heard this, He said, This sickness is not to end in death, but for the glory of God, so that the Son of God may be glorified by it."

Colossians 2:15 (NIV)

"And having spoiled principalities and powers, he made a shew of them openly, triumphing over them in it"

Revelation 21:4 (NIV)

"He will wipe every tear from their eyes. There will be no more death or mourning or crying or pain, for the old order of things has passed away."

1. Father, I declare that I will live and not die, to declare the works of the Lord. I pray for strength and vitality in my body, and for the energy to fulfill the purpose You have for my life.
2. Lord, I declare that I am healed by the stripes of Jesus Christ. I reject every symptom of sickness or disease that may be trying to attack my body. I pray that Your healing power would flow through me and make me whole.
3. Father, I trust in Your promises of protection and deliverance. I pray that You would surround me with Your angels, and keep me safe from all harm. I declare that no weapon formed against me shall prosper, and I will live to fulfill the destiny You have for my life.
4. Lord, I reject every spirit of death that may be lurking around my life and family. I pray that Your divine power would destroy every plan and scheme of the enemy to bring death and destruction into my life.
5. Father, I ask for Your protection over my loved ones and family members. Keep them safe from sickness,

disease, and the threat of death. Cover them with Your divine protection and keep them under the shadow of Your wings.

6. Lord, I pray that You would give me a strong immune system that can fight off any disease or sickness that tries to come my way. Strengthen me from within, and give me the courage to stand against sickness and death.
7. Heavenly Father, I come to You today to ask for Your divine protection over my life. I pray that You shield me from sickness and disease, and keep me safe from all harm. In Jesus' name, I pray. Amen.

22

VICTORY IN THE NAME OF JESUS

1 Corinthians 15:57 (NIV)

"But thanks be to God! He gives us the victory through our Lord Jesus Christ."

Philippians 2:10-11 (NIV)

"That at the name of Jesus every knee should bow, in heaven and on earth and under the earth, and every tongue acknowledge that Jesus Christ is Lord, to the glory of God the Father."

Romans 8:37 (NIV)

"No, in all these things we are more than conquerors through him who loved us."

John 16:33 (NIV)

"I have told you these things, so that in me you may have peace. In this world you will have trouble. But take heart! I have overcome the world."

John 8:36 (NIV)

"So if the Son sets you free, you will be free indeed."

1. Heavenly Father, I thank You for the victory that is found in the name of Jesus. I declare that I am more than a conqueror through Him who loves me, and I embrace the victory that You have secured for me on the cross.
2. Father, I thank You for the ultimate victory over death that Jesus achieved through His resurrection. I embrace the hope of eternal life and victory over every circumstance, knowing that nothing can separate me from Your love. In the name of Jesus, I stand firm, confident that I will overcome every challenge and experience victory in every area of my life.
3. Lord, I pray that You would strengthen my faith in the power of Your name. Help me to fully understand and believe that at the mention of the name of Jesus, every knee shall bow and every tongue confess that He is Lord.
4. Heavenly Father, I ask for victory over sin and temptation in my life. I renounce every sinful desire and submit myself to the authority of Jesus' name. Empower me by Your Spirit to walk in holiness and righteousness.
5. Lord, I pray for victory over the schemes of the enemy. I declare that no weapon formed against me shall prosper, and every tongue that rises against me in judgment, I shall condemn. Your name is my refuge and fortress, and in it, I find security and triumph.

6. Father, I surrender every area of my life to You and invite the power of Jesus' name to reign in every situation. I declare that in His name, I am set free from bondage, fear, and every form of oppression.
7. Lord, I pray for victory in my relationships and interactions with others. May the love of Christ flow through me, enabling me to forgive, reconcile, and extend grace to those who have wronged me. In Jesus' name, I overcome bitterness, resentment, and discord. In Jesus' name, I pray. Amen.

23

DESTROYING THE POWER OF THE SINFUL NATURE

Romans 6:6-7 (NIV)

"For we know that our old self was crucified with Him so that the body ruled by sin might be done away with, that we should no longer be slaves to sin—because anyone who has died has been set free from sin."

2 Corinthians 5:17 (NIV)

"Therefore, if anyone is in Christ, the new creation has come: The old has gone, the new is here!"

Galatians 5:16 (NIV)

"So I say, walk by the Spirit, and you will not gratify the desires of the flesh."

Galatians 5:24 (NIV)

"Those who belong to Christ Jesus have crucified the flesh with its passions and desires."

Colossians 3:5 (NIV)

"Put to death, therefore, whatever belongs to your earthly nature: sexual immorality, impurity, lust, evil desires and greed, which is idolatry."

1. Heavenly Father, I come before You today, acknowledging my need for Your help to destroy the power of the sinful nature in my life. I confess that I cannot overcome it on my own, but I trust in Your grace and strength to bring about transformation.
2. Lord, I pray for the power of Your Holy Spirit to work within me, convicting me of sin and empowering me to resist its pull. Help me to recognize the areas of my life where the sinful nature has taken hold, and give me the courage to confront and overcome them.
3. Father, I renounce the power of the sinful nature over my thoughts, words, and actions. I ask for Your forgiveness and cleansing, knowing that through Jesus' sacrifice on the cross, I have been set free from the bondage of sin.
4. Lord, I pray for a renewed mind and a transformed heart. Help me to meditate on Your Word and fill my thoughts with things that are pure, lovely, and praiseworthy. Strengthen me to resist the temptations that arise from the sinful nature.
5. Heavenly Father, I ask for Your guidance and wisdom in making choices that align with Your will. Give me

discernment to recognize the enticements of the sinful nature and the strength to choose righteousness and obedience instead.

6. Lord, I pray for accountability and support in my journey of destroying the power of the sinful nature. Surround me with fellow believers who will encourage and challenge me to walk in holiness, and help me to be open and vulnerable with them.
7. Father, I thank You for the victory that is found in Jesus Christ. I declare that His death and resurrection have broken the power of sin over my life. I trust in Your promise that I am a new creation in Christ, and I rely on Your grace and power to continually destroy the power of the sinful nature within me. In Jesus' name, I pray. Amen.

24
FRUIT OF THE SPIRIT

Galatians 5:22-23 (NIV)
"But the fruit of the Spirit is love, joy, peace, forbearance, kindness, goodness, faithfulness, gentleness and self-control. Against such things there is no law."

John 14:26 (NIV)
"But the Advocate, the Holy Spirit, whom the Father will send in my name, will teach you all things and will remind you of everything I have said to you."

1 Corinthians 13:13 (NIV)
"And now these three remain: faith, hope, and love. But the greatest of these is love."

Colossians 1:10 (NIV)
"So that you may live a life worthy of the Lord and please him in every way: bearing fruit in every good work, growing in the knowledge of God."

Ephesians 5:9 (NIV)
"(for the fruit of the light consists in all goodness, righteousness and truth)"

1. Heavenly Father, I thank You for the gift of the Holy Spirit who dwells within me. I pray that You would cultivate and manifest the fruit of the Spirit in my life in increasing measure.
2. Lord, I ask for an abundance of love to flow from my heart, that I may love You with all my being and love others selflessly and unconditionally.
3. Father, I pray for joy that surpasses circumstances, a deep-seated joy that is rooted in knowing You and experiencing Your presence.
4. Holy Spirit, I ask for an overflow of peace in my life, a peace that surpasses all understanding, guarding my heart and mind in Christ Jesus.
5. Lord, I pray for patience and long-suffering, that I may exhibit a spirit of endurance and forbearance in difficult situations and relationships.
6. Heavenly Father, I ask for kindness and goodness to characterize my interactions with others. Help me to extend grace, compassion, and acts of kindness in both word and deed.
7. Father, I pray for faithfulness and self-control, that I may be steadfast in my commitment to You and disciplined in every area of my life. Strengthen me to resist temptation and walk in obedience to Your will. In Jesus' name, I pray. Amen.

25

MORE THAN CONQUERORS

Romans 8:31-39 (NIV)

"No, in all these things we are more than conquerors through Him who loved us."

Philippians 4:13 (NIV)

"I can do all this through Him who gives me strength."

Isaiah 54:17 (NIV)

"No weapon forged against you will prevail, and you will refute every tongue that accuses you. This is the heritage of the servants of the Lord, and this is their vindication from me," declares the Lord."

1 John 4:4 (NIV)

"Little children, you are from God and have overcome them, for he who is in you is greater than he who is in the world."

Revelation 12:11 (NIV)

"And they have conquered him by the blood of the Lamb and by the word of their testimony, for they loved not their lives even unto death."

1. Heavenly Father, I thank You for the promise that I am more than a conqueror through Christ Jesus. Help me to fully embrace this truth and live with confidence in Your victory.
2. Father, I thank You for the assurance that nothing can separate me from Your love. In all things, I am more than a conqueror through Him who loves me. I embrace the abundant life You have promised and walk in the victory that is mine in Christ Jesus.
3. Lord, I surrender my fears, doubts, and insecurities to You. Strengthen me with Your power and remind me that I have the authority to overcome every obstacle and challenge that comes my way.
4. Lord, I declare that no weapon formed against me shall prosper. I reject every lie, accusation, and attack of the enemy. By the power of Your Spirit, I stand firm and victorious in every battle.
5. Father, I pray for a mindset of victory. Help me to see every trial and setback as an opportunity for growth and transformation. Fill me with unwavering faith that I can overcome any situation because You are with me.
6. Heavenly Father, I ask for Your guidance and wisdom as I navigate through life's challenges. Lead me in the paths of righteousness and show me the strategies and solutions that will lead to victory in every aspect of my life.

7. Lord, I pray for supernatural strength to persevere in the face of adversity. Help me to keep pressing forward, even when circumstances seem overwhelming. I trust in Your grace to sustain me and empower me to overcome. In Jesus' name, I pray. Amen.

26

DESTINY RECOVERY

Proverbs 3:5-6 (NIV)

"Trust in the Lord with all your heart and lean not on your own understanding; in all your ways submit to Him, and He will make your paths straight."

Jeremiah 29:11 (NIV)

"For I know the plans I have for you," declares the Lord, "plans to prosper you and not to harm you, plans to give you hope and a future."

Hebrews 11:3 (NIV)

"By faith we understand that the universe was formed at God's command, so that what is seen was not made out of what was visible."

Jeremiah 1:5 (NIV)

"Before I formed you in the womb I knew you, before you were born I set you apart; I appointed you as a prophet to the nations."

Isaiah 46:10 (NIV)

"I make known the end from the beginning, from ancient times, what is still to come. I say, My purpose will stand, and I will do all that I please."

1. Heavenly Father, I come before You with a humble heart, seeking Your guidance and wisdom in framing my destiny according to Your perfect plan for my life.
2. Lord, I surrender my own desires and ambitions to You, trusting that Your plans for me are greater than anything I could imagine. Help me to align my thoughts and aspirations with Your will.
3. Father, I ask for clarity and discernment in understanding the unique purpose and calling You have placed on my life. Show me the path I should take and empower me to walk in obedience to Your leading.
4. Lord, I pray for divine connections and opportunities that will open doors and propel me toward my destiny. Surround me with mentors, friends, and supporters who will inspire and encourage me along the way.
5. Heavenly Father, I surrender my fears and doubts to You. Strengthen my faith and help me to trust in Your provision and guidance as I step into the unknown and pursue the destiny You have ordained for me.
6. Lord, I pray for perseverance and resilience in the face of challenges and setbacks. Teach me to embrace them

as opportunities for growth and character development, knowing that You are working all things together for my good.

7. Father, I thank You for the assurance that You will fulfill the good work You have begun in me. Help me to walk with confidence and faith, knowing that as I seek You and follow Your leading, my destiny will be fulfilled according to Your perfect timing. In Jesus' name, I pray. Amen.

27

OVERCOMING FEAR

2 Timothy 1:7 (NIV)

"For God has not given us a spirit of fear, but of power and of love and of a sound mind."

Isaiah 41:10 (NIV)

"So do not fear, for I am with you; do not be dismayed, for I am your God. I will strengthen you and help you; I will uphold you with my righteous right hand."

Psalm 34:4 (NIV)

"I sought the Lord, and he answered me; he delivered me from all my fears."

Joshua 1:9 (NIV)

" Have I not commanded you? Be strong and courageous. Do not be afraid; do not be discouraged, for the Lord your God will be with you wherever you go."

1 John 4:18 (NIV)

" There is no fear in love. But perfect love drives out fear, because fear has to do with punishment. The one who fears is not made perfect in love."

1. Heavenly Father, I come to You in the midst of my fear and anxiety, seeking Your help and strength to overcome. I surrender my fears to You, knowing that You are the One who can bring peace and deliverance.
2. Lord, I confess that fear has held me back from stepping into the fullness of the life You have called me to. I ask for Your forgiveness and healing from the grip of fear that has hindered my progress.
3. Father, I pray for Your perfect love to cast out all fear from my heart. Help me to fully grasp the depth of Your love for me, knowing that Your perfect love drives out fear and brings me into a place of confidence and trust in You.
4. Lord, I ask for Your Holy Spirit to empower me to overcome fear. Fill me with Your peace that surpasses all understanding and give me the courage to face my fears head-on, knowing that You are with me.
5. Heavenly Father, I declare that I am not defined by fear but by faith in You. I choose to stand on Your promises and declare Your truth over my life, replacing every fearful thought with faith-filled declarations.
6. Lord, I pray for a renewed mindset that is focused on Your goodness and faithfulness. Help me to meditate on Your Word and fill my thoughts with Your promises, so that fear has no room to take root in my mind.

7. Father, I thank You for the victory I have in Jesus Christ. I declare that I am an overcomer, and fear has no power over me. I trust in Your strength and guidance to navigate through every fearful situation, knowing that You are leading me into a life of freedom and courage. In Jesus' name, I pray. Amen.

28
BREAKING GENERATIONAL PATTERNS

Ezekiel 18:20 (NIV)
"The one who sins is the one who will die. The child will not share the guilt of the parent, nor will the parent share the guilt of the child…"

Galatians 3:13-14 (NIV)
"Christ redeemed us from the curse of the law by becoming a curse for us, for it is written: Cursed is everyone who is hung on a cross..."

2 Corinthians 5:17 (NIV)
"Therefore, if anyone is in Christ, the new creation has come: The old has gone, the new is here!"

Exodus 20:6 (NIV)
"But showing love to a thousand generations of those who love me and keep my commandments."

Joel 2:25-26 (NIV)
"I will repay you for the years the locusts have eaten... You will have plenty to eat, until you are full, and you will praise the name of the Lord your God, who has worked wonders for you."

1. Heavenly Father, I thank You for Your mercy and grace that bring healing and restoration. I declare Your power over my family and my life, trusting that You are breaking every cycle of generational patterns and replacing them with Your blessings, peace, and abundance.
2. Lord, I confess any generational patterns of sin, dysfunction, or brokenness that have been passed down through my family line. I ask for Your forgiveness and cleansing, knowing that in You, there is freedom and the power to break these destructive cycles.
3. Father, I pray for discernment and insight to identify the root causes of the generational problems in my family. Help me to understand the patterns and behaviors that need to be addressed and transformed by Your Spirit.
4. Lord, I surrender these generational problems to You, knowing that I cannot overcome them on my own. I ask for Your strength and wisdom to navigate through the healing process and bring lasting change to my family line.
5. Heavenly Father, I intercede on behalf of my family members who have been affected by these generational issues. I pray for their healing, deliverance, and transformation. May Your love and grace touch their hearts and bring restoration to their lives.
6. Lord, I declare Your promises of generational blessing and redemption over my family. I believe that You are

able to turn the curses into blessings and bring about a new legacy of righteousness, peace, and joy.

7. Father, I thank You for the victory I have in Jesus Christ. I declare that in Him, I am a new creation, and the power of the generational problems has been broken. I trust in Your faithfulness to bring healing, wholeness, and generational restoration to my family. In Jesus' name, I pray. Amen.

29

DESTROYING EVIL ALTARS

2 Corinthians 10:4 (NIV)

"The weapons we fight with are not the weapons of the world. On the contrary, they have divine power to demolish strongholds."

Matthew 18:18 (NIV)

"Truly I tell you, whatever you bind on earth will be bound in heaven, and whatever you loose on earth will be loosed in heaven."

Colossians 2:15 (NIV)

"And having disarmed the powers and authorities, He made a public spectacle of them, triumphing over them by the cross."

Revelations 12:11 (NIV)

"They triumphed over him by the blood of the Lamb and by the word of their testimony; they did not love their lives so much as to shrink from death."

1 Kings 18:37-39 (NIV)

"Hear me, O Lord, hear me, that this people may know that thou art the Lord God, and that thou hast turned their heart back again..."

1. Heavenly Father, I come before You with gratitude for Your power and authority over all things. I thank You for Your guidance and protection as I walk in Your light, breaking free from any influences that do not align with Your will for my life and the lives of those connected to me. I rejoice in Your victory and declare Your blessings and freedom over us.

2. Lord, I renounce any conscious or unconscious participation in or connection to evil altars. I ask for Your forgiveness and cleansing, knowing that in You, there is redemption and freedom from all forms of darkness.

3. Father, I pray for discernment and revelation to identify any evil altars that have been set up against me or my family. Unveil their hidden strategies and expose their destructive influence, so that I may take appropriate spiritual action.

4. Lord, I stand in the authority and power of Jesus Christ to break the power of evil altars. I declare that no weapon formed against me shall prosper, and I decree that every evil assignment and influence directed toward me is nullified by the blood of Jesus.

5. Heavenly Father, I plead the blood of Jesus over every area of my life and the lives of my loved ones. I pray for a divine hedge of protection around us, shielding us from the schemes and attacks of evil altars.

6. Lord, I ask for Your Holy Spirit to guide me in spiritual warfare against evil altars. Grant me wisdom, discernment, and the right strategies to dismantle and destroy their works, bringing freedom, deliverance, and healing.
7. Father, I thank You for the victory I have in Christ Jesus. I declare that I am more than a conqueror through Him who loves me, and no evil altar can prevail against the power of Your name. I trust in Your unfailing love and protection as I walk in obedience and victory. In Jesus' name, I pray. Amen.

30
DESTROYING CURSES

Proverbs 26:2 (NIV)

"Like a fluttering sparrow or a darting swallow, an undeserved curse does not come to rest."

Luke 9:1 (NIV)

"And he called the twelve together and gave them power and authority over all demons and to cure diseases."

Galatians 3:13 (NIV)

"Christ redeemed us from the curse of the law by becoming a curse for us, for it is written: Cursed is everyone who is hung on a cross."

Luke 10:19 (NIV)

" I have given you authority to trample on snakes and scorpions and to overcome all the power of the enemy; nothing will harm you."

2 Corinthians 10:4 (NIV)

" The weapons we fight with are not the weapons of the world. On the contrary, they have divine power to demolish strongholds."

1. Heavenly Father, I come before You today to break every curse that has been spoken over my life, my family, and my future generations. I declare that every curse is null and void in the mighty name of Jesus.
2. Lord Jesus, I repent of any sin or wrongdoing that may have opened the door to these curses. I ask for Your forgiveness and Your cleansing blood to wash away every curse from my life and my family's life.
3. I plead the blood of Jesus over myself, my family, and my possessions, declaring that no curse can penetrate the powerful blood of Jesus.
4. I pray for wisdom and discernment to identify any hidden curses or demonic strongholds that may be operating in my life. Give me the strength to break free from them and to live a life of abundance and freedom.
5. Father God, I declare that I am a child of God, and no curse or evil plan of the enemy can prosper against me. I break every curse of poverty, sickness, and failure in the mighty name of Jesus.
6. I command every demonic force and every evil spirit that has been sent to hinder my life and progress to be destroyed and sent back to the pit of hell where they belong.

7. I declare that from this moment on, my life is filled with the blessings of the Lord. I am free from every curse and every negative influence. I am walking in the abundance of God's love, peace, and prosperity. In Jesus' name, I pray. Amen.

31

RETURN TO SENDER

Psalm 7:15-16 (NIV)

"He made a pit, and digged it, and is fallen into the ditch which he made. His mischief shall return upon his own head, and his violent dealing shall come down upon his own pate."

Ecclesiastes 10:8 (NIV)

"Whoever digs a pit may fall into it; whoever breaks through a wall may be bitten by a snake."

Psalm 35:7-8 (NIV)

"For without cause have they hid for me their net in a pit, which without cause they have digged for my soul. Let destruction come upon him at unawares; and let his net that he hath hid catch himself: into that very destruction let him fall."

Proverbs 26:27 (NIV)

"Whoever digs a pit will fall into it; if someone rolls a stone, it will roll back on them."

Matthew 18:18 (NIV)

"Truly I tell you, whatever you bind on earth will be bound in heaven, and whatever you loose on earth will be loosed in heaven."

1. Heavenly Father, I come before You in the name of Jesus, declaring that every attack, scheme, or evil sent against me or my loved ones is returned back to the sender. I release it with the authority I have in Christ.
2. Lord, I ask for Your divine protection and covering over my life. Surround me with Your heavenly hosts, thwarting every plot and plan of the enemy, and ensuring that nothing can harm me.
3. Father, I forgive those who have wronged me and release them from any judgment or retaliation. Instead, I commit them into Your hands, trusting that You are the ultimate judge and that You will deal with them justly.
4. I plead the blood of Jesus over every area of my life, sealing it from any form of evil or harm. Let the blood of Jesus act as a barrier, preventing any curses, attacks, or negative influences from entering my life.
5. Lord, I declare that no weapon formed against me shall prosper. Every tongue that rises against me in judgment is condemned. I stand firm in the assurance that You are my shield and my refuge.
6. Father, I pray for discernment and wisdom to recognize any hidden attacks or snares that the enemy may set for me. Open my eyes to see and understand the tactics of the enemy, enabling me to counter them with Your truth and power.

7. I proclaim victory in every area of my life. By the authority of Jesus Christ, I nullify and render powerless every plan, curse, or attack that the enemy has devised against me. I am more than a conqueror through Christ who strengthens me. In Jesus' name, I pray. Amen.

32

THE SPIRIT OF ERROR

John 17:17 (NIV)

"Sanctify them by the truth; your word is truth."

2 Timothy 2:15 (NIV)

"Do your best to present yourself to God as one approved, a worker who does not need to be ashamed and who correctly handles the word of truth."

John 16:13 (NIV)

"But when he, the Spirit of truth, comes, he will guide you into all the truth. He will not speak on his own; he will speak only what he hears, and he will tell you what is yet to come."

James 1:5 (NIV)

"If any of you lacks wisdom, you should ask God, who gives generously to all without finding fault, and it will be given to you."

Psalm 119:105 (NIV)

"Your word is a lamp for my feet, a light on my path."

1. Heavenly Father, I come before You acknowledging that Your Word is truth and that error has no place in my life. I pray for discernment and wisdom to recognize and reject every form of error that may come my way.

2. Lord, I ask for Your guidance and illumination as I study Your Word. Help me to understand it accurately and to discern any false teachings or misleading interpretations. Grant me a spirit of discernment to distinguish between truth and error.

3. Father, I surrender my thoughts, beliefs, and opinions to Your truth. Remove any preconceived notions or biases that may cloud my understanding. Fill my mind with Your truth, so that I may walk in alignment with Your will.

4. Lord, I pray for protection against the influence of false teachers and deceptive doctrines. Shield me from the allure of teachings that contradict Your Word. Give me a discerning heart and a spirit of conviction to stand firmly on Your truth.

5. Heavenly Father, I ask for Your grace and humility to correct any errors in my own beliefs or actions. Help me to be open to correction and willing to grow in my understanding of Your truth. Lead me in the path of righteousness and away from any form of error.

6. Lord, I intercede for those who are deceived by error.

I pray that You would open their eyes to the truth, that they may be set free from falsehood and brought into a deeper knowledge of Your Word. Use me, Lord, as a vessel of truth and love to help lead them to You.

7. Father, I commit myself to be a student of Your Word, to meditate on it day and night, and to let it shape my beliefs and actions. Fill me with Your Holy Spirit, who is the Spirit of truth, so that I may discern and reject error in all its forms. In Jesus' name, I pray. Amen.

33
FREEDOM FROM ANCESTRAL BONDAGE

Galatians 5:1 (NIV)

"It is for freedom that Christ has set us free. Stand firm, then, and do not let yourselves be burdened again by a yoke of slavery."

Psalm 107:14 (NIV)

"He brought them out of darkness, the utter darkness, and broke away their chains."

2 Corinthians 5:17 (NIV)

" Therefore, if anyone is in Christ, the new creation has come: The old has gone, the new is here!."

Colossians 2:14 (NIV)

" Having canceled the charge of our legal indebtedness, which stood against us and condemned us; he has taken it away, nailing it to the cross."

Isaiah 61:1 (NIV)

"The Spirit of the Sovereign Lord is on me because the Lord has anointed me to proclaim good news to the poor. He has sent me to bind up the brokenhearted, to proclaim freedom for the captives and release from darkness for the prisoners."

1. Heavenly Father, I come before You with gratitude for the blessings and freedom You have made available to me. I embrace Your power to transform and break any generational patterns, and I trust in Your divine intervention to lead me into a life of fullness, freedom, and purpose.
2. Lord, I repent on behalf of myself and my ancestors for any sins, idolatry, or disobedience that has contributed to the bondage in our bloodline. I ask for Your forgiveness and cleansing, breaking the power of these generational curses.
3. Father, I declare my identity as a child of God and a new creation in Christ Jesus. I renounce and break any ungodly soul ties, spiritual attachments, or unhealthy patterns that have been inherited from my ancestors. I release myself from their influence and claim my freedom in Christ.
4. Lord, I pray for the power of the Holy Spirit to operate in my life, breaking every chain of bondage that has plagued my family line. I ask for Your supernatural

intervention to sever and dismantle every generational curse, releasing me and future generations from their grip.

5. Heavenly Father, I plead the blood of Jesus over my life and the lives of my ancestors. I ask that the power of His blood would cleanse and purify our bloodline, redeeming every area that has been under the influence of ancestral bondage.
6. Lord, I invite Your light into the hidden places of my family history. Expose and reveal any areas that need to be addressed and healed. Bring restoration, reconciliation, and freedom to every broken and wounded part of my lineage.
7. Father, I thank You for the victory I have in Christ Jesus. I stand firm in the authority and power that You have given me. I declare my freedom from ancestral bondage and walk in the fullness of Your blessings and promises. In Jesus' name, I pray. Amen.

34

DIVINE RECOVERY

Joel 2:25 (NIV)

"I will repay you for the years the locusts have eaten—the great locust and the young locust, the other locusts and the locust swarm—my great army that I sent among you."

Jeremiah 30:17 (NIV)

"But I will restore you to health and heal your wounds," declares the Lord, "because you are called an outcast, Zion for whom no one cares."

Isaiah 61:7 (NIV)

"Instead of your shame you will receive a double portion, and instead of disgrace you will rejoice in your inheritance. And so you will inherit a double portion in your land, and everlasting joy will be yours."

1 Peter 5:10 (NIV)

"And the God of all grace, who called you to his eternal glory in Christ, after you have suffered a little while, will himself restore you and make you strong, firm and steadfast."

Psalm 147:3 (NIV)

"He heals the brokenhearted and binds up their wounds."

1. Heavenly Father, I come before You with a humble heart, acknowledging that I am in need of Your divine recovery. I surrender every area of my life that needs restoration and ask for Your healing touch.
2. Lord, I confess any sins, mistakes, or wrong choices that have contributed to my current state of brokenness. I ask for Your forgiveness and restoration. Wash me clean and renew my spirit, that I may walk in the fullness of Your grace.
3. Father, I pray for divine healing in my physical body. Restore every organ, tissue, and cell to perfect health according to Your perfect will. I declare that by the stripes of Jesus, I am healed, and I receive Your divine healing power to manifest in my body.
4. Lord, I ask for divine recovery in my emotional well-being. Heal my broken heart, mend my wounded spirit, and restore my joy. Fill me with Your peace that surpasses all understanding, and help me to release any bitterness, anger, or unforgiveness.
5. Heavenly Father, I seek divine recovery in my relationships. Restore and reconcile any broken or strained relationships in my life. Bring healing and unity where there has been division, and guide me in extending forgiveness and love to those who have hurt me.

6. Lord, I pray for divine recovery in my finances. Release Your abundance and provision into my life. Open doors of opportunity, restore what has been lost or stolen, and bless the work of my hands. Teach me to be a faithful steward of the resources You entrust to me.

7. Father, I surrender my dreams, ambitions, and plans to You. I trust that You have a divine purpose for my life, and I ask for Your guidance and direction. Lead me on the path of divine recovery, where I can experience the fullness of Your blessings and walk in alignment with Your will. In Jesus' name, I pray. Amen.

35

RESTORATION OF LIBERTY

John 8:36 (NIV)

"So if the Son sets you free, you will be free indeed."

2 Corinthians 3:17 (NIV)

"Now the Lord is the Spirit, and where the Spirit of the Lord is, there is freedom."

Galatians 5:1 (NIV)

"It is for freedom that Christ has set us free. Stand firm, then, and do not let yourselves be burdened again by a yoke of slavery."

Psalm 146:7 (NIV)

"He upholds the cause of the oppressed and gives food to the hungry. The Lord sets prisoners free."

Isaiah 61:1 (NIV)

"The Spirit of the Sovereign Lord is on me because the Lord has anointed me to proclaim good news to the poor. He has sent me to bind up the brokenhearted, to proclaim freedom for the captives and release from darkness for the prisoners."

1. Heavenly Father, I come before You, recognizing the areas of my life where I have experienced bondage and the loss of liberty. I surrender these areas to You and ask for Your restoration and freedom.
2. Lord, I confess any sins or wrong choices that have contributed to the loss of my liberty. I ask for Your forgiveness and cleansing. Set me free from the guilt and shame that have held me captive, and restore to me the joy of Your salvation.
3. Father, I pray for the restoration of my spiritual liberty. Break every chain that has bound me and hindered my relationship with You. Help me to walk in the fullness of Your truth, embracing the freedom that comes from knowing and serving You.
4. Lord, I seek restoration of my emotional and mental liberty. Heal the wounds and scars that have affected my thoughts and emotions. Release me from anxiety, fear, and negative patterns of thinking. Fill me with Your peace and renew my mind with Your truth.
5. Heavenly Father, I pray for the restoration of my relational liberty. Mend and reconcile broken relationships, both with You and with others. Help me to forgive and be forgiven, to love unconditionally, and to experience healthy and thriving connections.
6. Lord, I ask for the restoration of my physical liberty.

Heal and strengthen my body, removing any limitations or ailments that have hindered my ability to live and move freely. Grant me the vitality and energy to fulfill Your purposes for my life.

7. Father, I surrender my plans and desires to You, trusting in Your divine restoration. Lead me on the path of liberty and guide me into the abundant life You have prepared for me. I declare that I am restored in Christ and I walk in the freedom that He has secured for me. In Jesus' name, I pray. Amen.

36

RESTORATION OF PEACE

Isaiah 26:3 (NIV)

"You will keep in perfect peace those whose minds are steadfast because they trust in you."

Philippians 4:7 (NIV)

" And the peace of God, which transcends all understanding, will guard your hearts and your minds in Christ Jesus."

Isaiah 26:3 (NIV)

" Now may the Lord of peace himself give you peace at all times and in every way. The Lord be with all of you."

Psalm 85:8 (NIV)

"I will listen to what God the Lord says; he promises peace to his people, his faithful servants—but let them not turn to folly."

John 14:27 (NIV)

"Peace I leave with you; my peace I give you. I do not give to you as the world gives. Do not let your hearts be troubled and do not be afraid."

1. Heavenly Father, I come before You with a heart full of gratitude, trusting in Your presence and peace. I release all worries, anxieties, and fears into Your hands, and I invite Your restoration of perfect peace into my life.

2. Lord, I confess any areas of my life where I have allowed chaos or discord to take root. I repent of striving in my own strength and surrender to Your perfect peace that surpasses all understanding.

3. Father, I pray for the restoration of peace in my mind and thoughts. Renew my mind with Your truth and fill me with Your peace that guards my heart and mind in Christ Jesus. Help me to cast down every anxious thought and bring every concern to You in prayer.

4. Lord, I seek the restoration of peace in my relationships. Heal broken relationships, resolve conflicts, and bring harmony where there is discord. Help me to extend forgiveness, grace, and understanding to others, fostering an atmosphere of peace in my interactions.

5. Heavenly Father, I ask for the restoration of peace in my emotions. Calm the storms within me and bring healing to any wounds or traumas that have disrupted my peace. Fill me with Your joy and the assurance of Your presence, enabling me to navigate life's challenges with peace.

6. Lord, I pray for the restoration of peace in my circumstances. Bring order and stability to the areas of

my life that feel chaotic or unsettled. Help me to trust in Your sovereign control and rest in the assurance that You are working all things together for my good.

7. Father, I surrender my worries, burdens, and concerns to You, knowing that You are the Prince of Peace. I invite Your peace to dwell within me, to guard my heart and mind, and to guide my steps. I declare that Your peace will reign in every aspect of my life, and I receive the restoration of peace that comes from knowing You. In Jesus' name, I pray. Amen.

37

RESTORATION OF JOY

Psalm 51:12 (NIV)

"Restore to me the joy of your salvation and grant me a willing spirit, to sustain me."

Nehemiah 8:10 (NIV)

"Restore to me the joy of your salvation and grant me a willing spirit, to sustain me."

Isaiah 61:3 (NIV)

" And provide for those who grieve in Zion—to bestow on them a crown of beauty instead of ashes, the oil of joy instead of mourning, and a garment of praise instead of a spirit of despair."

Psalm 30:11 (NIV)

"You turned my wailing into dancing; you removed my sackcloth and clothed me with joy."

Romans 15:13 (NIV)

"May the God of hope fill you with all joy and peace as you trust in him, so that you may overflow with hope by the power of the Holy Spirit."

1. Heavenly Father, I come before You with a heart full of gratitude, trusting in Your ability to bring joy into my life. I surrender any heaviness or struggles I may be facing, and I invite Your restoration and peace to fill me with Your abundant joy.

2. Lord, I confess any areas of my life where I have allowed negativity, worry, or fear to overshadow my joy. I repent of dwelling on the negative and choose to focus on Your goodness and faithfulness.

3. Father, I pray for the restoration of joy in my heart. Heal the wounds and hurts that have stolen my joy and replace them with Your overflowing love and grace. Fill me with the joy of Your salvation and the assurance of Your presence.

4. Lord, I seek the restoration of joy in my relationships. Mend broken relationships, foster unity, and bring laughter and joy into my interactions with others. Help me to cultivate an atmosphere of joy and positivity in my connections.

5. Heavenly Father, I ask for the restoration of joy in my daily life. Help me to find joy in the small blessings and simple pleasures that You provide. Open my eyes to the beauty around me and remind me of Your goodness in every circumstance.

6. Lord, I pray for the restoration of joy in my purpose and calling. Renew my passion for serving You and using

my gifts and talents for Your glory. Restore the joy of pursuing Your will and experiencing the fulfillment that comes from walking in alignment with Your plans.

7. Father, I surrender my worries, anxieties, and concerns to You, and I choose to trust in Your unfailing love and faithfulness. I declare that joy is being restored in my life, and I receive the joy of the Lord as my strength. I will rejoice in You always, knowing that Your joy is my source of strength and hope. In Jesus' name, I pray. Amen.

38

SOUND HEALTH AND MIND

3 John 1:2 (NIV)

"Beloved, I pray that all may go well with you and that you may be in good health, as it goes well with your soul."

Proverbs 3:7-8 (NIV)

"Do not be wise in your own eyes; fear the Lord and shun evil. This will bring health to your body and nourishment to your bones."

Isaiah 26:3 (NIV)

"You will keep in perfect peace those whose minds are steadfast, because they trust in You."

Philippians 4:7 (NIV)

"And the peace of God, which surpasses all understanding, will guard your hearts and your minds in Christ Jesus."

2 Timothy 1:7 (NIV)

"For God gave us a spirit not of fear but of power and love and sound mind."

1. Heavenly Father, I come before You with a grateful heart for the gift of life and the desire for sound health and a sound mind. I surrender my physical and mental well-being to You, knowing that You are the ultimate healer and source of wisdom.
2. Lord, I pray for the restoration and preservation of my physical health. I ask for strength, vitality, and resilience in my body. Heal any illnesses, diseases, or infirmities that may be affecting me, and grant me the wisdom to make choices that promote good health.
3. Father, I ask for clarity and peace in my mind. Deliver me from anxiety, fear, and negative thoughts. Renew my mind and grant me the ability to think clearly, make wise decisions, and have a sound perspective on life.
4. Lord, I pray for protection against mental and emotional struggles. Guard my mind and heart from stress, depression, and any form of mental illness. Fill me with Your peace and joy that surpasses all understanding.
5. Heavenly Father, I ask for divine wisdom and discernment in taking care of my physical and mental well-being. Guide me in making choices that promote a healthy lifestyle, including proper nutrition, exercise, rest, and self-care.
6. Lord, I pray for the guidance and wisdom of medical professionals. Grant them insight and knowledge to provide accurate diagnoses and effective treatments.

Bless the hands of those involved in healthcare, and surround me with a supportive and caring healthcare team.

7. Father, I thank You for the promise of soundness of mind and health in Your Word. Help me to align my thoughts and actions with Your truth. Fill me with Your Spirit and empower me to live a life that glorifies You in both my physical and mental well-being. In Jesus' name, I pray. Amen.

39

SEASONS OF NEW THINGS

2 Corinthians 5:17 (NIV)

"Therefore, if anyone is in Christ, the new creation has come: The old has gone, the new is here!"

Isaiah 43:19 (NIV)

"See, I am doing a new thing! Now it springs up; do you not perceive it? I am making a way in the wilderness and streams in the wasteland."

Revelation 21:5 (NIV)

"He who was seated on the throne said, 'I am making everything new!' Then he said, 'Write this down, for these words are trustworthy and true.'"

Ezekiel 36:26 (NIV)

"I will give you a new heart and put a new spirit in you; I will remove from you your heart of stone and give you a heart of flesh."

Philippians 3:13-14 (NIV)

"Brothers and sisters, I do not consider myself yet to have taken hold of it. But one thing I do: Forgetting what is behind and straining toward what is ahead, I press on toward the goal to win the prize for which God has called me heavenward in Christ Jesus."

1. Heavenly Father, I thank You for the seasons of new things that You bring into my life. I surrender my expectations and plans to You, trusting in Your perfect timing and divine purpose.
2. Lord, I pray for an open heart and an open mind to receive the new things You have in store for me. Help me to let go of the old and embrace the fresh opportunities, experiences, and relationships You bring my way.
3. Father, I ask for wisdom and discernment to recognize the new things You are orchestrating in my life. Give me clarity and understanding to discern Your voice and follow Your leading in every season of change.
4. Lord, I pray for courage and boldness to step into the new things You have prepared for me. Strengthen my faith and remove any fears or doubts that may hinder me from embracing the blessings and breakthroughs You have in store for me.
5. Heavenly Father, I surrender my comfort zone to You and ask for the grace to embrace the challenges and growth that come with new seasons. Help me to let

go of what is familiar and step into the unknown with confidence, knowing that You are with me.

6. Lord, I pray for divine provision and abundance in every new season. Open doors of opportunity, provide for my needs, and grant me favor as I navigate the new paths and ventures You have set before me.
7. Father, I thank You for the promise of new things in Your Word. I declare that I am ready and willing to receive and embrace the new things You have ordained for me. I trust in Your faithfulness and believe that Your plans for me are good. In Jesus' name, I pray. Amen.

40

SHOWERS OF BLESSING

Deuteronomy 28:12 (NIV)

"The Lord will open the heavens, the storehouse of His bounty, to send rain on your land in season and to bless all the work of your hands. You will lend to many nations but will borrow from none."

Malachi 3:10 (NIV)

"Bring the whole tithe into the storehouse, that there may be food in my house. Test me in this," says the Lord Almighty, "and see if I will not throw open the floodgates of heaven and pour out so much blessing that there will not be room enough to store it."

Numbers 6:24-26 (NIV)

"The Lord bless you and keep you; the Lord make his face shine on you and be gracious to you; the Lord turn his face toward you and give you peace."

Psalm 67:1-2 (NIV)

"May God be gracious to us and bless us and make his face shine on us—so that your ways may be known on earth, your salvation among all nations."

Ephesians 3:20-21 (NIV)

"Now to him who is able to do immeasurably more than all we ask or imagine, according to his power that is at work within us, to him be glory in the church and in Christ Jesus throughout all generations, forever and ever! Amen."

1. Heavenly Father, I come before You with a heart of gratitude, acknowledging Your abundant blessings in my life. I surrender my desires and expectations to You, knowing that You are the source of all blessings.
2. Lord, I pray for showers of blessing to pour upon every area of my life. Rain down Your favor, provision, and goodness in abundance. Open the windows of heaven and pour out blessings that I cannot contain.
3. Father, I ask for a fresh outpouring of Your blessings upon my relationships. Heal and restore broken connections, bring unity and harmony, and fill my interactions with love, joy, and peace.
4. Lord, I pray for showers of blessing upon my finances. Release financial breakthroughs, increase my resources, and grant me wisdom to steward Your blessings with integrity and generosity.
5. Heavenly Father, I ask for showers of blessing upon my health and well-being. Bring healing and restoration to any areas of sickness or pain. Strengthen me physically, mentally, and emotionally, that I may live a life of vitality and purpose.

6. Lord, I pray for showers of blessing upon my dreams, aspirations, and endeavors. Open doors of opportunity, grant me divine favor, and empower me to walk in the fullness of my calling and potential.

7. Father, I thank You for the promise of showers of blessing in Your Word. I declare that I am a recipient of Your abundant blessings. I receive with gratitude and humility, and I commit to using Your blessings to bless others and bring glory to Your name. In Jesus' name, I pray. Amen.

41

SUCCESS OF CHILDREN

Deuteronomy 6:6-7 (NIV)

"And these words that I command you today shall be on your heart. You shall teach them diligently to your children, and shall talk of them when you sit in your house, and when you walk by the way, and when you lie down, and when you rise."

Proverbs 22:6 (NIV)

"Train up a child in the way he should go; even when he is old he will not depart from it."

Ephesians 6:1-3 (NIV)

"Children, obey your parents in the Lord, for this is right. 'Honor your father and mother' (this is the first commandment with a promise), 'that it may go well with you and that you may live long in the land.'"

Jeremiah 29:11 (NIV)

" For I know the plans I have for you," declares the Lord, "plans to prosper you and not to harm you, plans to give you a hope and a future."

Isaiah 54:13 (NIV)

"All your children will be taught by the Lord, and great will be their peace."

1. Heavenly Father, I come before You with a heart full of love and concern for the success and well-being of my children. I entrust them into Your loving care and ask for Your guidance and blessings upon their lives.
2. Lord, I pray for wisdom and discernment to be imparted to my children. Help them make wise choices, seek knowledge, and develop a hunger for learning and growth in all areas of their lives.
3. Father, I ask for protection over my children. Shield them from harm, both physically and spiritually. Surround them with godly influences and guard them against negative peer pressure and harmful temptations.
4. Lord, I pray for the development of character and integrity in my children. Help them to be honest, compassionate, and respectful towards others. Instill in them a strong work ethic and a heart of service.
5. Heavenly Father, I pray for the fulfillment of my children's dreams and aspirations. Guide them in discovering their talents and passions, and grant them opportunities to pursue their goals with diligence and perseverance.

6. Lord, I ask for healthy relationships for my children. Surround them with friends who will uplift and encourage them. May their relationships be built on love, trust, and mutual respect.
7. Father, I commit my children's future into Your hands. Help them to walk in obedience to Your Word and to trust in Your plans for their lives. May they find their ultimate success in loving and serving You. In Jesus' name, I pray. Amen.

42

BUSINESSES AND CAREER SUCCESS

Proverbs 16:3 (NIV)

"Commit your work to the Lord, and your plans will be established."

Proverbs 12:11 (NIV)

"Whoever works his land will have plenty of bread, but he who follows worthless pursuits lacks sense."

Proverbs 3:5-6 (NIV)

"Trust in the Lord with all your heart, and do not lean on your own understanding. In all your ways acknowledge him, and he will make straight your paths."

James 1:5 (NIV)

" If any of you lacks wisdom, let him ask of God, who gives to all liberally and without reproach, and it will be given to him."

Proverbs 13:20 (NIV)

" Walk with the wise and become wise, for a companion of fools suffers harm."

1. Heavenly Father, I come before You with a heart full of gratitude for the opportunities and abilities You have given me in my career and business endeavors. I commit my work and aspirations to You, seeking Your guidance and blessings.
2. Lord, I pray for wisdom and discernment in my business decisions. Help me to make choices that align with Your will and honor You. Grant me insights and creative ideas to excel in my field and to be a blessing to others through my work.
3. Father, I ask for favor and success in my business ventures. Open doors of opportunity and connect me with the right clients, partners, and resources. May my work be fruitful and impactful, bringing glory to Your name.
4. Lord, I pray for integrity and honesty in all my business dealings. Guard my heart against greed, dishonesty, and unethical practices. Help me to be a person of integrity, always seeking to do what is right and fair.
5. Heavenly Father, I ask for perseverance and resilience in the face of challenges and setbacks. Strengthen my faith and grant me the determination to overcome obstacles and press forward in my career and business pursuits.
6. Lord, I pray for divine connections and networking opportunities. Surround me with like-minded

individuals who can mentor, inspire, and support me on my professional journey. May we encourage and uplift one another in our pursuits.

7. Father, I surrender the outcomes of my career and business to You. Help me to trust in Your divine plan and timing. Grant me contentment and peace, knowing that my ultimate success is found in fulfilling Your purposes and bringing glory to Your name. In Jesus' name, I pray. Amen.

43
LIFE PARTNER

Proverbs 18:22 (NIV)

"He who finds a wife finds a good thing and obtains favor from the Lord."

Proverbs 19:14 (NIV)

"Houses and wealth are inherited from parents, but a prudent wife is from the Lord."

Psalm 37:4 (NIV)

"Delight yourself in the Lord, and he will give you the desires of your heart."

Proverbs 3:5-6 (NIV)

" Trust in the Lord with all your heart and lean not on your own understanding; in all your ways submit to Him, and He will make your paths straight."

2 Corinthians 6:14 (NIV)

" Do not be yoked together with unbelievers. For what do righteousness and wickedness have in common? Or what fellowship can light have with darkness?"

1. Heavenly Father, I come before You with a desire to find a life partner who is in alignment with Your perfect will for my life. I surrender my desires and preferences to You, trusting that You know what is best for me.
2. Lord, I pray for guidance and discernment in the search for a life partner. Open my eyes to recognize the person who will complement and support me in my journey of faith and purpose.
3. Father, I ask for a life partner who shares my values, beliefs, and commitment to serving You. May we grow together in our love for You and in our desire to live a life that honors You.
4. Lord, I pray for a life partner who will bring joy, love, and companionship into my life. May our relationship be built on trust, respect, and mutual support, and may we always seek to uplift and encourage one another.
5. Heavenly Father, I ask for a life partner who will walk alongside me in both the joys and challenges of life. Grant us the strength to face trials together and the ability to provide comfort and support to one another.
6. Lord, I pray for a life partner who will help me grow and become the best version of myself. May we inspire and motivate each other to pursue our dreams and fulfill our God-given purposes.

7. Father, I trust in Your perfect timing and divine orchestration. Help me to wait for the right person patiently and to use this season of singleness to grow closer to You. May I find contentment and fulfillment in You, knowing that You are working all things for my good. In Jesus' name, I pray. Amen.

44
FRUIT OF THE WOMB

Psalm 127:3 (NIV)

"Children are a heritage from the Lord, offspring a reward from him."

Genesis 1:28 (NIV)

"God blessed them and said to them, 'Be fruitful and increase in number; fill the earth and subdue it."

Exodus 23:26 (NIV)

"None shall miscarry or be barren in your land; I will fulfill the number of your days."

Deuteronomy 7:13 (NIV)

"And he will love you, bless you, and multiply you…"

Psalm 128:3 (NIV)

"Your wife will be like a fruitful vine within your house; your children will be like olive shoots around your table."

1. Heavenly Father, I come before You with a deep desire for the blessing of children. I surrender my longing for a child into Your hands and trust in Your perfect timing and plan for my life.
2. Lord, I pray for the gift of fertility and the ability to conceive. Heal any physical, emotional, or hormonal imbalances that may be hindering conception. Grant me and my spouse the grace to embrace the journey with patience and faith.
3. Father, I ask for protection over the life growing within me. Safeguard the health and development of the child, and surround us with Your divine presence and peace throughout the pregnancy.
4. Lord, I pray for strength and perseverance during any difficulties or challenges that may arise on this journey. Help me to trust in Your sovereignty and to lean on Your promises in times of uncertainty or disappointment.
5. Heavenly Father, I pray for the grace to surrender my desires and expectations to You. Grant me peace and contentment, knowing that Your plans are perfect, even if they differ from my own.
6. Lord, I ask for support and understanding from loved ones and the community around me. Help them to show compassion, sensitivity, and encouragement during this season of longing and waiting.

7. Father, I trust in Your unfailing love and faithfulness. Regardless of the outcome, I know that You have a purpose and a plan for my life. Grant me the grace to embrace Your will and to find joy and fulfillment in serving You, whatever the circumstances. In Jesus' name, I pray. Amen.

45
THE CHURCH

Matthew 16:18 (NIV)

"And I tell you that you are Peter, and on this rock I will build my church, and the gates of Hades will not overcome it."

Colossians 4:3 (NIV)

"And pray for us, too, that God may open a door for our message, so that we may proclaim the mystery of Christ, for which I am in chains."

Ephesians 4:1-3 (NIV)

"I, therefore, a prisoner for the Lord, urge you to walk in a manner worthy of the calling to which you have been called, with all humility and gentleness, with patience, bearing with one another in love, eager to maintain the unity of the Spirit in the bond of peace."

2 Chronicles 7:14-15 (NIV)

"If my people who are called by my name humble themselves, and pray and seek my face and turn from their wicked ways, then I will hear from heaven and will forgive their sin and heal their land. Now my eyes will be open and my ears attentive to the prayer that is made in this place."

Romans 12:5 (NIV)

"So we, though many, are one body in Christ, and individually members one of another."

1. Heavenly Father, I pray for the church, the body of Christ, to experience a fresh outpouring of Your Spirit. May Your presence fill every gathering, leading us into deeper intimacy with You and transforming lives.
2. Lord, I lift up the church's leaders before You. Grant them wisdom, discernment, and boldness to lead according to Your will. Equip them with Your anointing to preach the Word with power and to shepherd Your flock with love and compassion.
3. Father, I pray for unity within the church. Help us to set aside our differences and come together in love, supporting and encouraging one another. May our unity be a testimony to the world of Your transformative power.
4. Lord, I intercede for the spiritual growth and maturity of every member of the church. Stir up a hunger for Your Word and a passion for prayer in our hearts. Deepen our understanding of Your truth and empower us to live out our faith daily.
5. Heavenly Father, I pray for the church to be a beacon of hope and love in our community. Fill us with compassion for the lost and broken, and ignite a passion for evangelism and outreach. Use us to share Your love

and to bring salvation and healing to those who are in need.

6. Lord, I ask for Your divine protection over the church. Guard us from the attacks of the enemy and keep us safe from every scheme or strategy aimed at hindering Your work. Surround us with Your heavenly hosts and cover us with Your mighty hand.

7. Father, I pray for revival to sweep through the church, awakening hearts and igniting a fire for Your Kingdom. May Your Spirit move in power, bringing healing, deliverance, and transformation to lives. Use us, Lord, to impact our communities and to bring glory to Your name. In Jesus' name, I pray. Amen.

46

PASTORS AND PEOPLE IN MINISTRY

Ephesians 4:11-12 (NIV)

"And he gave the apostles, the prophets, the evangelists, the shepherds and teachers, to equip the saints for the work of ministry, for building up the body of Christ."

Ephesians 1:16-17 (NIV)

"I do not cease to give thanks for you, remembering you in my prayers, that the God of our Lord Jesus Christ, the Father of glory, may give you the Spirit of wisdom and of revelation in the knowledge of him."

Acts 14:23 (NIV)

"And when they had ordained them elders in every church, and had prayed with fasting, they commended them to the Lord, on whom they believed."

Acts 1:8 (NIV)

" But you will receive power when the Holy Spirit comes on you; and you will be my witnesses in Jerusalem, and in all Judea and Samaria, and to the ends of the earth."

1 Corinthians 1:10 (NIV)

"I appeal to you, brothers and sisters, in the name of our Lord Jesus Christ, that all of you agree with one another in what you say and that there be no divisions among you, but that you be perfectly united in mind and thought."

1. Heavenly Father, I lift up all pastors and people in ministry before You. Strengthen them in their calling and empower them with Your wisdom, grace, and anointing to fulfill their roles effectively.
2. Lord, I pray for a fresh infilling of Your Spirit upon pastors and people in ministry. Renew their passion, vision, and dedication to serving You and leading Your people. Fill them with boldness and confidence to proclaim Your Word.
3. Father, I ask for protection and covering over pastors and people in ministry. Guard them against spiritual attacks, discouragement, and burnout. Surround them with a community of support and provide them with godly mentors and accountability.
4. Lord, I pray for wisdom and discernment for pastors and people in ministry. Grant them insight into Your Word and the ability to rightly divide and apply it. Guide them in making decisions and leading with integrity and humility.
5. Heavenly Father, I intercede for pastors and people in ministry, asking for spiritual growth and personal revival

in their lives. Help them to prioritize their relationship with You above all else and deepen their intimacy with You.

6. Lord, I pray for unity and harmony among pastors and people in ministry. May they work together as a team, supporting and encouraging one another, and exemplifying the love and unity of the body of Christ.
7. Father, I thank You for pastors and people in ministry who selflessly serve Your Kingdom. I ask for provision and blessings in their personal lives and families. Strengthen their marriages, protect their children, and grant them rest and refreshment in their times of need. In Jesus' name, I pray. Amen.

47

MISSIONARIES AND MISSIONS

Matthew 28:19 (NIV)

" Therefore go and make disciples of all nations, baptizing them in the name of the Father and of the Son and of the Holy Spirit, and teaching them to obey everything I have commanded you. And surely I am with you always, to the very end of the age."

Luke 10:2 (NIV)

"The harvest truly is great, but the laborers are few; therefore, pray the Lord of the harvest to send out laborers into His harvest."

Acts 1:8 (NIV)

"But you will receive power when the Holy Spirit comes on you; and you will be my witnesses in Jerusalem, and in all Judea and Samaria, and to the ends of the earth."

Acts 13:47 (NIV)

" For this is what the Lord has commanded us: 'I have made you a light for the Gentiles, that you may bring salvation to the ends of the earth."

Romans 10:14-15 (NIV)

"How, then, can they call on the one they have not believed in? And how can they believe in the one of whom they have not heard? And how can they hear without someone preaching to them? And how can anyone preach unless they are sent? As it is written: 'How beautiful are the feet of those who bring good news!"

1. Heavenly Father, I lift up missionaries and missions before You, recognizing their vital role in spreading the Gospel to the ends of the earth. Strengthen them in their calling and provide them with wisdom, courage, and perseverance.
2. Lord, I pray for divine protection over missionaries as they go into unfamiliar and sometimes dangerous territories. Surround them with Your angels, shield them from harm, and grant them favor with the people they are ministering to.
3. Father, I ask for provision and resources for missionaries and missions. Supply their financial needs, open doors for partnerships and support, and enable them to carry out their work effectively.
4. Lord, I pray for spiritual breakthroughs in the lives of those being reached by missionaries. Open hearts to receive the Gospel, break down strongholds and barriers, and draw many to salvation and discipleship.
5. Heavenly Father, I intercede for missionaries' families who sacrifice and support them from behind the scenes.

Strengthen and protect their marriages, nurture their children, and provide them with a sense of security and peace.

6. Lord, I pray for unity and collaboration among missionaries and mission organizations. May they work together in harmony, supporting and encouraging one another, and leveraging their collective efforts for greater impact.
7. Father, I thank You for the dedication and sacrifice of missionaries who leave their homes and familiar surroundings to bring the good news of Jesus Christ to the nations. Pour out Your blessings upon them, refresh and renew their spirits, and grant them joy and fulfillment in their service. In Jesus' name, I pray. Amen.

48

LEADERS AND GOVERNMENT

Proverbs 8:15-16 (NIV)

"By me kings reign and rulers issue decrees that are just; by me princes govern, and nobles—all who rule on earth."

Romans 13:1 (NIV)

"Let every person be subject to the governing authorities. For there is no authority except from God, and those that exist have been instituted by God."

1 Timothy 2:1-2 (NIV)

"I urge, then, first of all, that petitions, prayers, intercession, and thanksgiving be made for all people— for kings and all those in authority, that we may live peaceful and quiet lives in all godliness and holiness."

Proverbs 21:1 (NIV)

"The king's heart is a stream of water in the hand of the Lord; he turns it wherever he will."

Daniel 2:21 (NIV)

"He changes times and seasons; he deposes kings and raises up others. He gives wisdom to the wise and knowledge to the discerning."

1. Heavenly Father, I lift up leaders and those in positions of authority before You. Grant them wisdom, discernment, and integrity to lead with righteousness and justice.
2. Lord, I pray for a spirit of humility and servant leadership to fill the hearts of leaders. Help them to prioritize the well-being of the people they serve above personal interests and ambitions.
3. Father, I ask for protection over leaders and their families. Shield them from harm, both physically and spiritually, and guard them against corruption, temptation, and attacks from the enemy.
4. Lord, I pray for unity and cooperation among leaders, that they may work together for the greater good of society. Break down walls of division, pride, and prejudice, and foster an atmosphere of collaboration and mutual respect.
5. Heavenly Father, I intercede for leaders' decision-making processes. Guide them in making just and compassionate choices that align with Your will and contribute to the welfare and progress of the people they govern.
6. Lord, I pray for leaders to be surrounded by wise

counselors and advisors who offer godly counsel and support. Grant them discernment to recognize and heed wise advice, and the humility to seek counsel when needed.

7. Father, I thank You for leaders and government officials who serve as instruments of Your authority. I pray that they may come to know You personally and seek Your guidance and wisdom in their leadership. Fill them with Your love, compassion, and mercy, that they may govern with a heart of service and stewardship. In Jesus' name, I pray. Amen.

49

NATIONS

Psalm 22:28 (NIV)

"For dominion belongs to the Lord and he rules over the nations."

Habakkuk 2:14 (NIV)

"For the earth will be filled with the knowledge of the glory of the Lord as the waters cover the sea."

Jeremiah 29:7 (NIV)

"Seek the welfare of the city where I have sent you into exile, and pray to the Lord on its behalf, for in its welfare you will find your welfare."

Proverbs 14:34 (NIV)

"Righteousness exalts a nation, but sin is a reproach to any people."

2 Chronicles 7:14 (NIV)

"If my people who are called by my name humble themselves, and pray and seek my face and turn from their wicked ways, then I will hear from heaven and will forgive their sin and heal their land."

1. Heavenly Father, I lift up the nations of the world before You. You are the Creator and Ruler of all nations, and I acknowledge Your sovereignty over them. May Your will be done on earth as it is in heaven.
2. Lord, I pray for the leaders of nations. Grant them wisdom, integrity, and a heart for the well-being of their people. Guide them in making decisions that promote peace, justice, and prosperity for all.
3. Father, I ask for unity and reconciliation among nations. Break down walls of division, prejudice, and animosity. Help leaders and citizens to seek understanding, common ground, and peaceful resolutions to conflicts.
4. Lord, I intercede for nations facing poverty, injustice, and oppression. Bring transformation and healing to those societies. Raise up leaders who will champion the cause of the marginalized and work towards equality and social justice.
5. Heavenly Father, I pray for the spiritual state of nations. Pour out Your Spirit upon the people, that they may turn to You in repentance and faith. Ignite a revival that will bring about transformation, righteousness, and a hunger for Your truth.
6. Lord, I pray for the protection and well-being of nations. Shield them from natural disasters, conflicts, and terrorism. Grant wisdom to leaders in handling

national security, and raise up peacemakers who will work towards reconciliation and harmony.

7. Father, I thank You for the diversity of nations and cultures. Help us to celebrate and appreciate one another's differences, fostering an atmosphere of respect, cooperation, and unity among nations. In Jesus' name, I pray. Amen.

50

MAKING HEAVEN

Matthew 7:13-14 (NIV)

"Enter through the narrow gate. For wide is the gate and broad is the road that leads to destruction, and many enter through it. But small is the gate and narrow the road that leads to life, and only a few find it."

John 14:6 (NIV)

"Jesus answered, 'I am the way and the truth and the life. No one comes to the Father except through me."

1 John 5:11-12 (NIV)

"And this is the testimony, that God gave us eternal life, and this life is in his Son. Whoever has the Son has life; whoever does not have the Son of God does not have life."

John 3:16 (NIV)

"For God so loved the world, that he gave his only Son, that whoever believes in him should not perish but have eternal life."

Ephesians 2:8-9 (NIV)

"For by grace you have been saved through faith. And this is not your own doing; it is the gift of God, not a result of works, so that no one may boast."

1. Heavenly Father, I come before You with a heart that longs to be with You in eternity. I surrender my life to You and seek Your guidance and grace to walk the path that leads to heaven.
2. Lord, I pray for a deep and personal relationship with You. Help me to know You intimately, to hear Your voice, and to follow Your will. Draw me closer to You every day and deepen my love for You.
3. Father, I repent of my sins and ask for Your forgiveness. Cleanse me and purify my heart so that I may be worthy to stand in Your presence. Help me to live a life that is pleasing to You and aligned with Your Word.
4. Lord, I ask for the guidance and empowerment of Your Holy Spirit. Lead me in righteousness, convict me of any wrongdoing, and empower me to live a life of holiness and obedience to Your commands.
5. Heavenly Father, I pray for strength and perseverance on my journey towards heaven. Help me to overcome trials, temptations, and distractions that seek to pull me away from You. Fill me with Your Spirit, that I may walk in the power and victory of Christ.
6. Lord, I seek Your grace and mercy. Cover me with Your

unfailing love and extend Your grace towards me. Help me to extend the same love and grace to others, sharing the hope of heaven with those around me.

7. Father, I fix my eyes on the eternal hope of heaven. Keep me focused on the prize, knowing that this life is temporary, but eternity with You is everlasting. Help me to live each day with an eternal perspective, investing my time, talents, and resources in things that matter in eternity. In Jesus' name, I pray. Amen.

www.ingramcontent.com/pod-product-compliance
Lightning Source LLC
LaVergne TN
LVHW020716110826
845149LV00012B/2282

* 9 7 8 1 9 5 7 8 0 9 8 6 1 *